Business Practice
for THERAPISTS

Business Practice for THERAPISTS

Nicola Jenkins

Hodder & Stoughton

A MEMBER OF THE HODDER HEADLINE GROUP

Orders: please contact Bookpoint Ltd, 130 Milton Park, Abingdon,
Oxon OX14 4SB. Telephone: (44) 01235 827720.
Fax: (44) 01235 400454. Lines are open from 9.00–6.00,
Monday to Saturday, with a 24 hour message answering service.
You can also order through our website hodderheadline.co.uk

British Library Cataloguing in Publication Data
A catalogue record for this title is available from the British Library

ISBN 0 340 876794

First Published 2003
Impression number   10 9 8 7 6 5 4 3 2 1
Year   2007 2006 2005 2004 2003

Typeset by Phoenix Photosetting, Chatham, Kent.
Printed in Great Britain for Hodder & Stoughton Educational,
a division of Hodder Headline Plc, 338 Euston Road, London
NW1 3BH by Arrowsmiths Ltd.

Contents

Acknowledgements

This book wouldn't have been possible without the support and insights of a lot of people along the way.

Thanks to all my past ITEC and VTCT students who asked really probing questions and helped me improve the way I developed my own work and thought about the therapeutic business – most of whom have thriving businesses of their own now.

A huge thanks to the expert witnesses – Julie, Helena, Lucy, Andrew, Astrid, Lesley, Trevor and Sarah for sharing their valuable insights, experiences and suggestions on how to be more effective at what we do.

Lastly, I owe a huge debt to Joanne, Anthony, Alan, Anne, Andrew and Drew for cups of tea, Chinese takeaways, listening ears, encouragement and 'pull yourself together' in equal amounts. I couldn't have done it without you.

What have you let yourself in for?

The complementary health and beauty markets are amongst the most rapidly growing industries worldwide. More people are turning to therapists for stress relief, emotional support and aid with various physical conditions each day and getting the support they came for. As interest grows in the benefits of each form of complementary therapy, so also does interest in training to become a therapist; which means more competition for clients and a lot of that competition comes from big companies. Just how much competition is there?

○ There are over 40,000 hairdressing/beauty therapy salons throughout the United Kingdom (UK)

○ Over 6 per cent of the total number of people employed in service industries work within health, hairdressing and beauty

○ There are over 45,000 freelance or mobile therapists

○ In 1999 it was estimated that £3,400m was spent on treatments received in salon environments – this figure does not include treatments spent in other venues (such as health centres, mobile treatments, airlines or similar).

(*Source: Hairdressing and Beauty Industry Authority*)

The growing number of practitioners does mean more competition, but there is a payoff: more people – and many influential people at that – are expressing interest in and approval of complementary therapies in general:

○ In the UK, people spend around £650 million on spa breaks each year (source www.epolitix.com), and more is spent in countries such as the USA and Canada.

○ An Institute of Management report for 1996 showed that around 270,000 people in the UK take time off each day for work-related stress. If you take NHS charges, sick pay and lost production into account, this adds up to £7 billion annually (source www.workstress.net).

○ One in five people in Britain use at least one type of complementary medicine each year (source: Ernst E, White A, The BBC survey of complementary medicine uses in the UK, *Complementary Therapies Medicine* 2000;8:32–36).

○ Researchers at Exeter University, in two separate studies, revealed that 46 per cent of UK doctors consider complementary therapies to be effective; a detailed survey of general practitioners in South West England discovered that 68 per cent of the respondents were involved with complementary therapies in some way during the previous week, 16 per cent of them practising a therapy themselves, 25 per cent referring at least one patient and 55 per cent endorsing a therapy. (White AR, Resch KL, Ernst E; Complementary Medicine: use and attitudes among GPs, *Family Practice* 1997; 14:302–306; Ernst et al, Complementary medicine. What physicians think of it: a meta analysis. *Arch Internal Medicine* 155(22): 2405–8 Dec 11–25 1995).

○ A survey of GPs in Canada showed that 73 per cent of those who responded wanted to know more about the major complementary therapies, and particularly about their use for chronic pain or illness and musculoskeletal problems. (Verhoef MJ, Sutherland LR, General practitioners' assessment of and interest in alternative medicine in Canada. *Social Science Medicine* 41(4) 511–515.

○ Over 60 per cent of Australian GPs want further training in complementary therapies with over 75 per cent of those surveyed having already formally referred a patient to a complementary therapist (*Australian Family Physician* 2000 June; 29(6): 602–6.

And what about the new therapists training each year? Whilst many are coming straight out of school, others are choosing to change from their existing careers with

○ 43 per cent saying they want to change careers in order to earn more money

○ 16 per cent wanting a new challenge

○ 13 per cent wanting to do something more fulfilling.

(Source: workthing.com – extract from 'Taking the plunge' survey of 1,000 workers published by Penna Sanders & Sidney Career Consulting, November 2001)

Where do you fit into the picture?

With interest in complementary therapies growing and more therapists receiving their qualifications each day, you have the potential to develop a career that is absorbing, fulfilling and personally challenging on every level.

However, earning a good living as a therapist is part of that challenge. As with any new business, it takes time to make it work, plus a clear idea of what you want to do and how you want to get there. Some therapists struggle for years without getting what they want from their business, usually because they haven't planned thoroughly, promoted appropriately or continued to make an effort with their marketing.

Perseverance, planning, enthusiasm and a love of your subject are essential qualities for success, as is the ability to promote yourself. This book seeks to help you through the initial steps and to encourage you to take a more active approach to making your business work. Work through the tasks in each chapter and you will come to a very thorough understanding of yourself, your clients, your business and where it can take you.

At the end of this chapter you should be able to

○ Provide a short definition of the key United Kingdom (UK) laws that could affect your work as a complementary therapist

○ Provide an explanation as to why these laws are important to your work

○ Explain the relevance of certain European Union (EU) Directives to your work

Introduction

The legal system exists to protect the interests and health and safety of clients and therapists as they go about their work. As a result, there are a number of laws that have an impact on the way in which we work and specifically cover issues such as:

○ how you promote your work

○ how you interact with your clients

○ how you interact with colleagues, your employer or (if you are the boss) with your employees

○ how your workplace is arranged

○ the use of equipment in the workplace

○ dealing with accidents and emergencies that take place at your place of work

○ dealing with suspicious waste products.

Failure to comply with these laws can jeopardise your position as a therapist. Firstly, these laws are often referred to when the different therapeutic associations or governing bodies set up their rules for membership – so to ignore them means that if a serious problem arose you may find yourself expelled from the organisation you are a member of, which usually means losing your professional status.

Secondly, it can invalidate your professional insurance, which means that should you be sued, you will have to pay the costs yourself.

The rules that govern the way we practise come from a number of sources:

○ Government Legislation – or Acts that have been approved by Parliament and provide us with the day-to-day regulations we need to work safely and effectively and to protect the interests of our clients.

○ EU Directives – the EU issues directives from time to time that are designed to encourage all member states of the EU to bring their own regulations in line with the standards set for the whole of Europe.

○ Local government – individual local authorities can specify particular ways in which the laws should be interpreted in their area. For instance, in one part of London it is illegal for female therapists to massage male clients either below the neck or above the knees without a special licence. In another borough, body treatments such as massage, reflexology, Indian head massage and similar can only take place between the hours of 9 am and 5 pm.

REFLECTION

What, if any, local government regulations exist in the area in which you wish to practise? How much does a licence cost in your area?

General health and safety

The Health and Safety Executive (HSE) is responsible for ensuring that health and safety laws are maintained by all businesses within the UK. Your local authority can send inspectors to visit your premises and are not required to give you notice of their visit. If, in the course of their visit, they discover any problems, they will initially issue an improvement notice, which gives you three weeks in which to make the changes they insist upon. If, however, the faults are serious or, on a return visit, they discover that the changes have not been made, they will issue a prohibition notice that means all business activity must be suspended until the problems are fixed.

The HSE and the Health or Environment Inspectors are interested in making sure the businesses visited comply with the following Acts:

Health and Safety at Work Act 1974

This protects your rights either as an employer or as an employee, and is relevant to all businesses, not just to therapists. The law states that the employer must

○ provide a safe working environment

○ provide training for staff about how to work safely in their environment

○ produce a written statement about the company's health and safety policy, which is clearly displayed and which all employees are made aware of

○ make sure that any clients, self-employed therapists (for instance those renting a room on the premises) or other visitors are not exposed to any health risks whilst on the premises.

Employees are expected to be careful whilst they work, help their employer to maintain these standards and not to do anything that might put their health, or anyone else's health, at risk.

Local Government (Miscellaneous Provisions) Act 1982

The local authority (the Environmental Health Department) is responsible for registering and licensing any businesses where invasive treatments, such as skin puncturing, take place on the premises. This includes all body piercing, ear piercing, tattooing, epilation, or acupuncture. Therapists practising disciplines such as colonic irrigation are also advised to register with their local authorities.

Visits from the Environmental Health Officer are designed to make sure that

○ all equipment is thoroughly and appropriately cleansed and sterilised

○ only fully qualified therapists are working there

○ waste products and any used needles are safely, hygienically and appropriately disposed of

○ the premises are kept scrupulously clean

○ the certificate of registration, indicating that you have met the required standards, is displayed.

The Management of Health and Safety at Work Regulations 1992

This act outlines the responsibilities of the owner/manager of a business to ensure that

○ they establish procedures that protect the health and well-being of all who visit their premises, to prevent accidents of any kind

○ they regularly check that the health of employees and clients is not being risked in any way

○ they keep a record of the checks they have made

○ they check those who work for them are properly trained to do so

○ they keep a record of any first aid treatment, and report accidents or diseases as appropriate.

The Workplace Regulations 1992

These regulations govern the appearance of all parts of the workplace, not just the treatment rooms. If the regulations are met, you can expect that the workplace

○ is clean and tidy, including all staff and client toilets, with hot and cold running water and adequate soap and towels (or similar)

○ is properly ventilated from windows or with clean air-conditioning

○ is well lit in all areas, even if you choose to work with lights dimmed during body treatments, you are able to control the lighting as required

○ is maintained at a comfortable temperature (at least 16° Celsius, although this will usually be marginally warmer if clients are expected to remove clothing)

○ is clear of all waste material (anything produced as a result of a treatment should be appropriately removed)

○ has up-to-date, appropriate fire-fighting equipment that is easily accessible and stored with instructions for use

○ has drinking water available

○ has a designated area for staff to change, rest and eat and where their clothing and belongings can be safely stored.

The Manual Handling Regulations 1992

Most of these regulations relate to appropriate posture when lifting and are designed to reduce the risk of injuries resulting from incorrect lifting, supporting and carrying of loads. These regulations require that you

○ learn how to safely carry out any manual tasks required in the workplace

○ find alternative ways of handling heavy or unwieldy loads

○ 'take reasonable care' when handling loads, bearing your own, and other people's safety in mind when doing so

○ use appropriate equipment to lift loads where it is available.

DISCUSSION

What kinds of manual handling do you engage in during the course of your work? What equipment is available to help you with this handling? How would you adapt your handling techniques if you were a) working from home; b) running a mobile service?

Products

Control of Substances Hazardous to Health Act (COSHH) 1989

This Act provides guidance on dealing with chemical substances that could enter the body and cause skin irritations, allergies or burns and potentially cause difficulties breathing or could be life-threatening. For the most part, this legislation is going to be relevant to therapists working in centres where chemical products are sold or where strong chemicals are stored or used on a regular basis and demands that both the employer and the employee (plus anyone working there on a self-employed basis) are aware of hazards and the safety measures that govern their use. The law requires that you

○ are aware of which substances could be dangerous

○ know what the health risks are

○ know what to do if an accident happens

○ create a code of conduct that will minimise the risk of an accident happening

○ train everyone so they are aware of what they have to do and why

○ regularly check that the rules are being followed

○ assess how effective these rules are and make amendments where necessary to make them more effective

○ handle and store chemicals in line with their manufacturer's instructions

○ ensure all substances are correctly labelled

○ dispose of used or out-of-date substances in a safe manner that does not harm the environment.

| TOXIC | HARMFUL |
| HIGHLY FLAMMABLE | CORROSIVE |

Figure 1.1 Hazard symbols

Assess your own working environment and answer the following questions:

(1) How many chemical substances are you aware of that could be classed as hazardous?

(2) What are these substances, and where are they stored?

(3) What would happen if someone were accidentally exposed to these substances?

(4) What first aid measures would have to be taken if exposure took place?

(5) What rules exist in your workplace to ensure that any risk to health from these substances is minimised?

(6) What checks are carried out to make sure everyone is following the rules?

FOR DISCUSSION

More accidents take place within the home than in any other environment. If you intend to carry out treatments from your home or as part of a mobile practice, what precautions can you take with respect to the storage and safe use of chemical substances? Hint: this is particularly relevant if you consider how and where your cleaning products are stored, if you practise beauty therapy or if you work with essential oils.

Equipment

The Provision and Use of Work Equipment Regulations 1992

These state that all equipment used must be

- in a good state of repair
- regularly maintained, with written records of its servicing and any required repairs
- correctly made for its purpose
- correctly used, by staff trained to use it effectively and appropriately.

DISCUSSION

What equipment are you trained to use that would need regular maintenance? What equipment could you learn to use that would enhance your work?

The Personal Protective Equipment at Work Regulations 1992

This Act requires that any member of staff who may be exposed to health risks is provided with the necessary protective equipment and that this equipment is

- provided free of charge
- is appropriate for the task at hand
- is properly maintained or replaced.

REFLECTION

What kinds of health risks are you exposed to in your work? What kinds of personal protection could you use to minimise these risks?

The Health and Safety (Display Screen Equipment) Regulations 1992

These regulations are relevant to anyone who works with computers and insist that you

- get regular eye tests paid for by your employer if you are not self-employed
- take regular breaks from your desk
- have a chair with adjustable height and back support
- can adjust the brightness and contrast of the screen.

Employers are also required to assess any problems you have with the equipment, such as flickering images, or the position of the unit or the lighting and come up with solutions that improve the situation for you. These can include providing anti-glare screens for computers, moving the work station, repairing the computer, adding tilt-and-swivel mechanisms to the screen, and much more.

The Electricity at Work Regulations 1992

These regulations govern the use of electrical equipment in the workplace and ensure that

○ any equipment is checked at least once a year by a qualified electrician

○ any faulty equipment is removed from service and immediately sent for repair

○ written records of tests are kept should an inspector wish to see them.

When an accident happens

Health and Safety (First Aid) Regulations 1981

No matter how small a business, there must be first aid treatment available should an injury take place. This means that

○ someone in the business who is on site most of the time knows how to administer first aid in the event of an accident and that they regularly update their first aid qualifications

○ there is a fully stocked first aid box available, which also contains guidance on how to treat the injured

○ notices are displayed that say where the first aid box is and who is responsible for first aid.

The majority of the governing bodies require that all complementary therapists registered with them continue to update their first aid skills on a regular basis. In a larger organisation, such as a health centre, sports centre, spa or salon environment, these regulations require that at least one member of staff undergo training in first aid.

There are strict rules about what should be stored in a first aid box, and it is very important that these regulations are adhered to for the safety of the injured and the therapist as well as to prevent any additional complications. In the first aid box, you should find

○ individually wrapped, sterile dressings of different sizes and shapes

○ wound cleansing sterile wipes

○ triangular bandages (which could be used, for instance, to produce slings)

○ sterile saline solution

○ disposable gloves

○ scissors

○ gauze

○ adhesive tape

○ safety pins

○ an information card, outlining how to proceed under certain conditions.

Your personal first aid box

A number of therapeutic disciplines promote the use of certain actions or substances as part of a first aid response – hence aromatherapists might tell you that lavender is good to apply for minor burns. What would you put into an alternative first aid kit and why? Don't forget to design the information card, making it easy to use.

Remember that this first aid kit does not replace the regulation first aid box and should not be stored near it.

RIDDOR – The Reporting of Injuries, Diseases and Dangerous Occurrences Regulations 1995

These regulations outline the correct procedure to adopt if a workplace accident occurs. It deals with the needs of a business to

○ have an accident book

○ ensure that any injury or dangerous occurrence is written into the accident book immediately after it happens with as many details as possible as to what happened. These details should include the time, date, place and nature of the event, the action taken, plus signatures for the therapist, the injured party and a witness (if possible)

○ report an accident to the local authority immediately by telephone and follow-up with a written report within 10 days, if the event involves a death, poisoning, electric shock or a major injury

○ act appropriately to deal with the situation, making the injured and the premises safe

○ keep all records of the incident for at least three years.

Fire Precautions (Workplace) Regulations 1997

These regulations ensure that the safety of all those present is considered and planned for should a fire take place. The regulations require that

○ a means of escape from the building is available and clearly marked

○ that the escape route is kept clear of obstructions (and that any fire doors are not locked)

○ that all fire fighting equipment is properly checked and maintained (this includes fire alarms, smoke alarms, fire blankets, fire extinguishers, and so on)

○ that the escape route and fire procedure are clearly displayed

○ that you know what to do if a fire takes place – how to raise the alarm, evacuate, where to find the equipment and how to use it and when not to try to fight the fire yourself

○ that you are aware of the different kinds of extinguishers, what they contain and when each one should be used.

DISCUSSION

Given the different types of fire extinguisher (listed below), which type or types would be best for you to buy if you were a) running your business from home; b) providing a mobile practice using your car; c) setting up a small practice in rooms within an office building. Where would you store these extinguishers?

COLOUR OF LABEL ON EXTINGUISHER	CONTENTS	USED FOR
Black	Carbon Dioxide	Electrical fires Burning liquid
Cream	Foam	Wood Paper Textiles Burning liquid
Blue	Powder	Wood Textiles Electrical fires Burning liquid
Red	Water	Wood Paper Textiles

Employment

Maternity/paternity

The Employment Act of 1982 and Social Security Act of 1996 give expectant parents certain rights. Until recently these were concerned primarily with the expectant mother and her rights to fair employment under law. New legislation now in place recognises the role of the father in child rearing and bearing and has simplified the existing legislation. These amendments affect all those with children expected to be born after 6 April 2003. The parents of these children have the following rights:

○ Paid time off for ante-natal care.

○ Maternity or paternity pay, during a period of leave due to the pregnancy and the confinement.

○ Time off for the pregnancy and confinement and to be allowed to return to work after this period of leave.

- Two weeks' compulsory leave immediately after the birth for the biological mother (not the adoptive mother).

- The mother's period of leave could be the newly extended statutory minimum of 26 weeks (in the UK), or longer – depending on any special arrangements offered by the company for whom the therapist works. If the therapist has been working for up to 26 weeks with the same company prior to the 15th week before their estimated week of childbirth, they are eligible for the full 26 weeks' leave and could make a case for getting any additional maternity/paternity benefits offered by that company.

- Adoptive parents are also eligible for the same rights.

- Parents can complain and seek redress through the appropriate authorities if unfairly dismissed as a result of pregnancy.

- Parents have the right to apply to work flexibly – this is for any parents with children aged under six or who have disabled children aged under 18. The employer has a duty to consider the request seriously.

- Paternity leave allows the father to take up to two weeks' paid leave to care for the new baby and support the mother. This is only on the condition that the father has or will have responsibility for the child's upbringing, is the biological father of the child or the mother's husband/partner and that they have been working continuously for their employer for 26 weeks leading to the 15th week before the baby is due.

- Paternity leave can either start from the date of the child's birth, or from a chosen date, as long as it is within 56 days of the actual birth.

- Fathers taking paternity leave will also be protected from unfair dismissal and can complain or seek redress if unfair dismissal on the grounds of paternity leave is suspected.

Dealing with your clients

Data Protection Act 1984

The Data Protection Act is only relevant to you if you are storing information about your clients on a computer. If you are, or intend to do so, you must

- register your business on the Data Protection Register

- state the kind of information you are storing, how it will be used and who has access to it

- keep it secure, accurate and relevant

- give clients access to the files you have about them if they wish to see them.

It is also a good idea to let clients know if you are planning to sell your business to a new therapist or if you have someone covering your business for a while (perhaps if you are going away for an extended period of time or if you intend to take maternity leave). This can reassure your clients that you have their interests at heart and give them the opportunity to let you know if they do not wish the new therapist to have access to information about them when s/he begins to take over your case load.

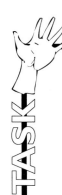

Because this Act relates specifically to the use of computers, many therapists choose to store their client records in other, secure filing systems and complete client notes by hand. Identify as many benefits and drawbacks to both methods of maintaining client records – either manually or on the computer – as you can.

Consumer Protection Act 1987

This is designed to look after your clients' interests and protect them from any product deemed unsafe. Any person who experiences damage or injury as a result of a product can seek redress from the manufacturers, producers and importers, but not from the wholesaler or retailer (unless they withhold the producer's/manufacturer's details when these are requested by the injured party). Any product that could potentially cause damage is open to scrutiny under this Act.

Sale and Supply of Goods Act 1994

This Act protects your clients' rights by insisting that any goods or services sold must be

○ of a satisfactory standard

○ suitable for the purpose(s) described

○ accurately described

○ provided in a reasonable time and for a reasonable price.

REFLECTION

What do you think a 'satisfactory standard' means for your therapy? How could you prove that you are working at that standard? What do you think a 'reasonable' time and price for your treatments would be? Are you able to work within this 'reasonable' timescale? What do you think an 'unreasonable' timescale and price for your treatment would be?

FOR DISCUSSION

If clients are dissatisfied with the service you offer (and wish to sue) but have not received any personal injury as a result of treatment, they are most likely to argue that you have broken either the Sale and Supply of Goods Act or the Trade Descriptions Act. What possible reasons can you think of for a client to sue the therapist with respect to these laws?

Trade Descriptions Act 1972

This Act is particularly relevant to therapists as it relates to how the goods or services are described in any kind of advertising or promotional material or in verbal descriptions given by the therapist or a colleague. The Act makes it illegal to mislead the public in any way and, with respect to complementary therapies, this usually refers to making false claims about what you, your treatments or your products are able to do. With respect to this

Act, pay particular attention when producing your promotional literature and promoting your services to ensure that you

○ do not claim to cure anything

○ avoid making price comparisons between your products/services and prices they have been offered at elsewhere

○ do not offer a 50 per cent discount on a product or service until after it has been available for 28 days at full price.

FOR DISCUSSION

Complementary therapies can be of huge benefit to clients suffering from a range of conditions. If you cannot claim to cure a condition, how could you effectively promote the benefits of the treatment you offer?

DISCUSSION

Given that discounting can be a great help at establishing client interest as you start up a business, how could you effectively use discounts at the beginning of your business and still not break the rules of the Trade Descriptions Act?

The changing face of legislation

The government and the European Union are constantly revisiting and revising the laws that govern the practice of complementary therapies. At the time of going to press, there were a number of recent changes and forthcoming laws that could have an effect on the way we practise in the future. Watch out for more details about the following:

The House of Lords 2000 report on complementary therapies

This report highlights the ways in which complementary therapies are becoming more widely available through the National Health Service (NHS) and makes suggestions as to what needs to happen in order for the therapies to become more effectively integrated into the health service. The various disciplines are divided into three groups, one of which contains those already in use through the NHS who are disciplined by self-regulating bodies (Osteopathy, Chiropractic, Homeopathy, Herbal Medicine and Acupuncture); the second group contains those where there is some provision within the NHS at the moment but where provision is not widespread (aromatherapy, Alexander Technique, stress management, hypnotherapy, reflexology, shiatsu); the third group includes those disciplines

that favour a philosophical approach that appears to the House of Lords to be at odds with the scientific principles on which conventional medicine is based (Ayurvedic, Traditional Chinese Medicine, crystal therapy, iridology, kinesiology).

European Directive on Food Supplements

This legislation is aimed at making sure vitamins and minerals sold as dietary supplements are standardised in terms of the information available to the consumer about them, that appropriate safety data is provided and that the consumer is not misled about the effects of the products in any way. The directive insists that

- detailed information about recommended daily consumption is provided on the label
- warnings about the effects of exceeding recommended daily limits must be included
- the products cannot claim to prevent, treat or cure illnesses
- the manufacturer/producer or retailer cannot say (or write) anything suggesting a varied diet does not provide the necessary nutrients
- any vitamins/minerals or other pills, which are sold in packaging that resembles pharmaceutical products, must bear the statement 'this is not a medicinal product'.

Traditional Herbal Medicinal Products Directive

This legislation recognises the increasing demand by consumers for herbal medicinal products and aims to introduce quality checks to bring herbal medicines in line with other conventional medicinal products, to propose a simplified registration procedure for herbal medicines and to recognise that, instead of insisting on new tests for these products, registration can be based on information about the medicine's traditional use over a period of at least 30 years, 15 of which must be within the EU.

Much of the interest and controversy surrounding this legislation relates to cases where herbal medicines are linked to unfortunate side effects when mixed with conventional medicines or where they can reduce the effectiveness of the prescribed medicine.

Own-brand, home-produced and non-European herbal products are currently exempt from licensing and sold as foods under Section 12 of the Medicines Act 1968. With the new legislation coming in, there is a possibility that home-produced medicines, as well as those that originate in the Americas, Asia or the Far East, may not be able to meet the new standards required by the EU and may no longer be available. Problems involved with herbs in the licensing process include

○ difficulty isolating the active ingredient(s)

○ difficulty defining exactly how the product works

○ the plants from which the products are derived can't be patented

○ no two products are going to be chemically the same, so theoretically each product (for instance a whole range of items containing St John's Wort) will each have to undergo separate testing and licensing.

EU Medicines Directive 1965/2001

The EU is making changes to the way in which it defines a medicinal product and to revisit the way in which medicinal products are licensed. The Traditional Herbal Medicines Directive is seen as being part of this directive. There is the possibility that certain food supplements and herbal preparations may be reclassified as medicines, which would mean that they would then have to comply with the licensing requirements expected of pharmaceutical drugs – a costly procedure. The key definitions introduced describe a medicine as anything that is

○ medicinal by presentation – so that a member of the public recognises that the substance is supposed to treat or prevent disease in humans or animals and that these claims are seen on labelling, packaging, through any promotional literature or through use of the media, **or**

○ medicinal by function – that the substance is understood to have active ingredients whose action is understood and can be explained scientifically as having certain risks and/or benefits.

Take a look at the illustration below. Which laws is this therapist breaking and how?

Figure 1.2 The work space of an untidy Therapist.

1. Who makes the rules under which we work?

2. What does the Health and Safety Executive do?

3. List three activities an employer must do to comply with the Health and Safety at Work Act.

4. What can you expect of your place of work if it is following the Workplace Regulations?

5. Outline your responsibilities as a therapist in view of the Manual Handling Regulations. How would this vary if you had to lift clients as part of your work?

6. Explain the regulations of the Control of Substances Hazardous to Health Act.

7. What must you do to comply with the Electricity at Work Regulations?

8. What precautions should you have in place in the event of an accident? Refer to the Health and Safety First Aid Regulations and RIDDOR.

9. What does RIDDOR stand for?

10. List the contents of a first aid box.

11. List the key aspects of the Fire Precautions Regulations.

12. What can a pregnant therapist expect to receive in terms of maternity benefits?

13. What can a male therapist receive in terms of paternity benefits?

14. What precautions must you take with respect to your clients' notes to stay in line with the Data Protection Act?

15. How could a therapist be in breach of the Trade Descriptions Act?

16. What is required of therapists under the Sale and Supply of Goods Act?

At the end of this chapter you should be able to

○ Design your own working space

○ Discover what, if any, local legislation affects your practice

○ Discuss the practical steps you may wish to take to manage interruptions and environmental pollution

○ Relate your working environment to the clients you wish to attract and their expectations

○ Discuss ways in which you could use display areas such as windows or reception areas to promote your products and services effectively

Introduction

At the beginning of their training courses, many student therapists tend to focus on the practical skills they are gaining above all else. Whilst the practical skills are essential, and your clients will come to you in order to receive the benefits of those skills, your treatment involves more than just the actions you are carrying out. The treatment involves your applying the knowledge you gained in order to assess how best to treat your client (or deciding when not to treat that client). It also involves the whole environment in which the treatment takes place. Your interaction with your environment is the focus of this chapter.

DEFINITION

Holism/holistic approach – this is open to a great deal of interpretation. A quick answer is that a holistic approach to treatment involves taking into consideration all aspects of the client's well-being, focussing on their body, mind, spirit and environment.

Your personal working space

How you interact with your working space is going to depend very heavily on how you intend to work (see chapter 8) and the amount of control you have over that space. Yet there are some common elements and the time may come when you find yourself with a free rein over how you will set up your workspace.

If you are in the process of designing a workspace, there are certain elements you need to consider:

○ Any regulations set out by your governing body and/or local authority as to the content or nature of the workspace. Some governing bodies may insist on hand-washing facilities being in the treatment room, rather than outside it, which can be difficult if you intend to work at home.

○ The access requirements of the clients you intend to treat. For instance, if you intend to work with physically frail or handicapped individuals, you may need to consider wheelchair access and/or practising from a ground floor room where there is no need to climb stairs.

○ Any privacy issues. This is particularly important if you are working from home. It is strongly advised that you do not practise your treatments from your bedroom as this, in particular, can be misinterpreted. In all environments you will also need to consider if the room is overlooked in any way and how you can protect the client's privacy during the treatment process.

○ Does the room have to be 'dual purpose'? If you work from home, having your treatment room function as something else, such as a guest or second bedroom, when you aren't using it, is a sensible idea as it allows you to avoid paying capital gains tax should you sell your home at a later date. If you intend to work out of the second bedroom in this way, you must make sure that its other function, as a bedroom, is not obvious to the client.

○ Exit/entry to the room. What access points are available? Can these be controlled in any way? If you are working in a family or home environment, can you take steps to make sure you are not interrupted during a treatment?

○ Lighting – whilst natural daylight is preferable in most cases, you will need to weigh this up against the client's need for privacy and ensure the treatment room isn't overlooked. If you are working in the evenings or in a space where daylight isn't available, bear in mind that lowered lighting is more relaxing to the client. The ability to control the lighting is strongly preferred. If your lighting choices are either 'on' or 'off', you may wish to consider changing the lightbulbs (if you are able to), or introducing uplighters or lamps to light the room in a creative and relaxing way.

○ Ventilation – this should be adequate so that the room has a regular supply of fresh air and that it smells fresh and inviting when the client arrives.

○ Heating – this must be appropriate to the client's comfort and the form of treatment you are carrying out, as well as meeting the appropriate regulations.

○ Decoration – clients will have different expectations of your working space depending on the venue you are practising from, anything they have heard about you and your particular form of treatment and may even form an impression from your leaflet. You may wish to consider asking your clients or potential clients about what they would like to see in a working space. Decoration in this case refers to the choice of paint, wallpaper, furniture and fittings. Pastel shades of paint or simple abstract designs on wallpaper are generally deemed to be more relaxing. If you have the choice or you want to add more colour to the treatment room, you can then consider using personal touches to add that colour. Furniture and fittings should be arranged so that they allow you to move freely and without obstruction around the room.

○ Personal touches – paintings, photographs, ornaments, books and similar can be used to convey a great deal about the way in which you practise. Generally, the more personal touches there are to a workspace, the more relaxing and comforting the place can be – as long as you don't let it become cluttered. For a thoroughly professional or clinical appearance, remove all personal touches or keep any decorations in the treatment rooms confined to plants, your framed qualifications and similar.

FOR DISCUSSION

Consider the impression you would like to make on your clients. How could you reflect this in your workspace?

FOR REFLECTION

What expectations would you have of the workspace(s) occupied by each of the following therapists:

○ one who is particularly interested in spiritual and emotional support and development

○ one who is focussing on sports injuries and rehabilitation

○ one who gets most of their business by referral from the local GPs

FOR DISCUSSION

What do you like/dislike about the clinic environments that you find yourself visiting? Consider those run by other therapists as well as your doctor or dentist's treatment rooms.

How, if at all, could a mobile therapist control their working space and/or decorate it?

Enhancing your treatment room with feng shui

The Chinese art of placement can have profound effects on the success of your business if you use it effectively. There are a large number of books on this subject if you wish to investigate it properly, but you could try it out on a small scale with your treatment room if you so desired. Key issues to consider are

○ remove all clutter, this includes dead/dying plants or dried flower arrangements – if you want easy-care plants, use silk flowers rather than dried ones

○ any plants you have in the treatment room should have soft rounded leaves

○ air the room regularly or ensure good ventilation

○ place your equipment and any personal touches (or cures) in the appropriate sectors of the bagua in order to enhance the success of your business.

Design a work room suitable for your treatment process, taking into account issues such as access for clients, toilet and washing facilities, and the layout of the room. What special equipment do you need? Is your design dependent on how you will use this equipment? Is the room intended for any other purpose?

Local authority licences

As discussed in chapter 1, your local authority regulates the practice of treatments in your area. Whilst the focus of their attention is predominantly on those disciplines involving invasive treatments, they can, and sometimes do, have rules relating to the practice of all complementary therapies. These rules exist for the safety of you and your clients as well as ensuring that you are practising in an ethical and appropriate manner. For the most part, the rules are in place to make sure that:

○ you are not using the therapeutic practice as a cover for prostitution

○ your working space is appropriate for the intended task, and complies with the Health and Safety and Workplace regulations

○ that you are fully and appropriately trained in the discipline you intend to practise

○ that you are properly insured (usually your insurance will depend on your having a licence – make sure you check this out with your insurers).

In certain circumstances you may be exempt from having to get a licence, usually if

○ you are a registered member of a recognised organisation or governing body and the governing body insists on a code of conduct for its members

- the governing body also requires continuing professional development from its members as well as requiring a specific standard of initial training prior to joining them

- the governing body requires you to have professional indemnity insurance

- clear disciplinary procedures exist in the governing body's regulations and by-laws.

Not every local authority will support or recognise the involvement of a governing body, preferring instead to check and approve each therapist individually. The onus does remain with you to find out how, if at all, your practice is affected.

TASK

Contact your local Environmental Health Office to find out about the rules governing the practice of complementary therapies in your area. What, if any, rules exist that could limit how and when you practise or the kinds of client you work with?

Managing your environment effectively

Whatever reasons your clients have for coming to you for treatment, their expectations of that treatment will include having your full attention for the duration of the treatment. Distractions of any kind are unwelcome and, if dealt with inappropriately, could

- encourage the client to go elsewhere for treatment

- make them lose their concentration so that they forget to give you information that could change the direction of the treatment

- make you lose your concentration so you forget to ask important questions

- reduce the rapport built between you and the client

- discourage them from confiding in you if they feel the need to talk.

Avoiding these distractions involves setting up systems that help to maintain the integrity of the treatment, the privacy of the client and allow you to keep your mind focussed solely on the client. These are especially important to bear in mind if you are working from home or as a mobile therapist.

Interruptions

- Use an answerphone or answering phone service – do not pick up the phone whilst you are carrying out a treatment.

- Any phone that you have in the treatment room should be switched off or turned to 'silent ringer' during the treatment.

- Ensure that all other users of the treatment venue understand that interruptions are unacceptable during the treatment. This may include putting a sign on the treatment room door saying that when it is shut, please wait quietly for attention (and/or direct clients to a waiting area).

- If working from home, ask other household members to avoid interrupting you and to remain quiet if treatment is in progress.

- Whilst interruptions are sometimes necessary, make sure that all those using the facilities understand what is meant by an 'emergency' or a necessary interruption. Make it clear that any other interruption is unacceptable.

- Arrange for some form of reception service, either by having a colleague responsible for dealing with enquiries or a friend/family member providing this service whilst you are working.

- If you anticipate certain problems, particularly personal problems, arising during the course of the treatment, take every step possible to ensure that those problems are dealt with either in advance of the treatment or afterwards. Remember that professional behaviour involves leaving your issues outside the treatment room and focussing on the client.

- In a professional environment, such as a salon, spa or similar, it is advised that you avoid personal calls at work as far as possible. You could use a mobile phone but switch it off, returning calls when you are less busy.

- Similarly, in a professional environment, it is possible to control other interruptions. Most interruptions are going to be requests for information or equipment. If you and your colleagues establish clear procedures (which could include setting up a manual for procedures or having a message board where you can display any changes to practice relevant for that day or week) you can avoid most interruptions. Any equipment that is held in common (for instance if you share an infra-red lamp or an ultrasound machine) must be returned to its storage space between treatments in order to avoid people interrupting all other practitioners whilst searching for it. In

these circumstances, you could also arrange to timetable clients in such a way that you avoid conflicting demands for equipment, or arrange that the equipment is only available to one therapist for a specific time period.

- Ask clients to switch off mobile phones as well.

- If you are doing a home visit, encourage the client to arrange that there are no interruptions during the treatment session. Use a room that will not be disturbed and unplug the phone if necessary.

Environmental pollution

Environmental pollution can take many forms and you may already be considering the effects of pollution on your client's health as part of the treatment you are providing them with. However, it is also important that you look at the ways in which your working environment could be protected from the most distracting and uncomfortable forms of environmental pollution: for the duration of the treatment, your client should, as far as possible, be free from the adverse effects their environment could have on them. The worst offenders (and the ones which you can do the most about) are listed below.

Noise

- If working in a busy street, with a lot of regular traffic, take steps to reduce the street noise, for instance by keeping the door to the centre closed.

- Play soft music to cover street noises or to aid the client's relaxation.

- Install a water feature near the entrance to the treatment centre to distract clients from street noises.

- Consider installing double-glazing if the noise is particularly bad.

- If working at home, make sure that all appliances, telephones and similar are turned off for the duration of the treatment.

- Encourage a quiet environment, this is particularly important if working from home.

Air pollution/fragrance

- Maintain high levels of personal hygiene, avoiding perfume or colognes where possible as these can be overpowering.

- Keep the treatment room properly ventilated, encouraging the flow of fresh air.

- Ensure that your working centre or treatment room is kept as a non-smoking environment and/or that you clean it thoroughly (including using air freshener) afterwards if someone has smoked in it.

- Use air freshener, essential oil steamers/vaporisers or similar to hide all other unpleasant smells. This includes animal smells and cooking smells if you are working from home or near a cafe.

Hygiene

- This is dealt with in more detail in chapter 9, however, all possible methods of hygiene are essential to keep the therapist, the treatment room, waiting area and the approach to the treatment centre as clean and welcoming as possible.

Lighting

- Lowered lighting is more relaxing (as mentioned above), installing dimmer switches is advisable where possible.

- Use daylight bulbs and avoid fluorescent overhead lights where possible.

- Get all lighting equipment regularly checked by an electrician. This is particularly important if there is a tendency for lights to flicker or be invasive.

- Allow natural daylight to enter the treatment room where possible, even if you then choose to shut curtains or blinds if the client needs to undress for the session.

Using display areas effectively

Every aspect of the treatment centre and workspace is on display when a client visits. Just as personal touches in the treatment room can enhance the appearance of the room and add to the impression the client has of you and your work, so these display areas can be used to

- enhance your professionalism

- provide the client with additional information about the nature and extent of your services

- attract the attention of passing clients (window displays and open waiting areas)

- advertise any special promotional events you are running

- display products for sale

- entertain clients whilst they wait for you

- offer suggestions for home care or after care advice – particularly useful if you are very busy and don't always have the time for an extensive after-treatment feedback session (this is often the case in professional environments, particularly where you are unlikely to get repeat visits from clients).

Anything constitutes a display area – you do not have to have lockable glass cabinets and floor to ceiling shelves to produce an effective display. Blank walls can support visual material; tables and creative shelving units can illustrate products and services and, in a professional environment, the window display is of paramount importance.

Blank walls are ideal for displaying your qualifications or any other elements that might enhance your reputation and your client's understanding of the services you can offer. You can also find leaflet holders, which can be wall-mounted or displayed on a flat service (perhaps in the reception area) to hold detailed information about the nature of your services.

Your waiting area can also be used to enhance your reputation when you include a folder of any positive publicity you've had or any clients' references or recommendations – saying how much they gained from the treatment (this is assuming that they are willing to write such a letter and for others to see it; you must ask permission from the client before doing this).

Information relating to the effectiveness of the treatment process as well as to any after care and home care is also useful in the waiting area. If you are selling books as part of your service, use one or two copies as display copies for people to read whilst they are waiting. Otherwise, a choice of recent magazines is always acceptable.

To make the most of your display area, think about it as a life size advertisement for your services. Just as with all advertising and promotional activities (see chapter 7), you want to

- attract attention
- hold interest
- create desire
- encourage action.

Doing this effectively is best achieved if you make the display area

- dynamic – create a sense of movement through the display, draw the eye in different directions, preferably towards the key product or message you are trying to get across

- changeable – change the display frequently – at least every couple of months, so clients returning to the area always have something new to look at. Any display material that is recycled needs to look new and clean for best effect. (Consider how often your favourite clothing shops change their window displays – you can learn from their practices too)

- topical – the most effective displays are those that relate events or circumstances going on in the outside world to the treatment process. For instance, you may wish to focus your displays on seasonal changes in the weather, or on people's activities. You could also incorporate references to well-publicised national events run by charities related to health issues, for instance quitting smoking, breast cancer awareness, AIDS awareness, National Back Pain week, or similar. If there are key sporting or other events going on in your local area, you can also incorporate references to these in your display

- eye-catching – position the display so that it is the first thing the client notices when they enter the treatment area; large images are particularly effective at drawing the eye

- clear – avoid making the display area cluttered or difficult to use and understand. Too many products or items in the display area can be overwhelming. If you have additional messages you want to get across, consider displaying them elsewhere, either on the walls or perhaps in a nearby leaflet stand

- colourful – use colour effectively to attract attention and to set off the products or messages appropriately; make sure the thing you want to sell (or say) most is aligned so that it draws the eye most readily

- cohesive – make sure the display follows a theme or looks pulled together. Aim for one key message that you are trying to get across, with all other elements of the display adding to that message. For instance, you may wish to 'take the stress out of Christmas' for your clients, and incorporate gift ideas, gift vouchers and additional treatment offers in your display. You could also use inexpensive materials related to your theme to enhance the message

○ professional – as far as possible avoid hand-lettering for any display posters or messages, keep the display area clean, dust-free and appropriately lit. Many product companies will also supply you with display stands or materials to enhance the appearance of your display area

○ three-dimensional – artistically stacked materials not only make the display area more visually interesting, but they also suggest that the products displayed are in great demand by others. If working with a shelf or table, you may also wish to dress the area using a plain tablecloth or piece of fabric. Dressing the area will also allow you to hide plain boxes or other items, which you can use to create a three-dimensional effect and which then function as stands to better display your key product or message.

The first time you create a visual display is always the hardest one to do, as it takes a while to get used to the equipment and space you are using and to focus on the way in which the client will see it. When you set up your display, draw back from it and look at it again from the first point at which the client could see it (think about the direction from which they arrive – is it always from the same point?). Stand back and ask yourself:

○ What do you notice first?

○ What message are you giving out?

○ Is the message clearly stated and visible?

○ How close do you have to be before you can read any written messages?

○ Is the display attractive and interesting? Will it make clients want to touch or handle the products (in which case it is working!)?

○ Will it bring about the reaction you desire from your preferred clients?

○ What other messages are also visible to the client from this point? Does your message stand out from the crowd? (Think about other shop windows nearby if you are working in a professional environment).

○ Do other messages in the treatment or waiting area enhance or distract from the display?

○ Does the display look cohesive and professional? Do you need to move anything to make it look more exciting?

○ Do you need to change the lighting on the display to make it more effective?

○ If the display is in a waiting area, is it clearly visible from the position(s) the clients are sitting in? (Consider where clients prefer to sit, there is usually a 'hot seat' which is the first choice of seat on entering the waiting area. Check where the display appears in relation to that seat or seats).

DISCUSSION

What kinds of thing could you put in a display to appropriately advertise your services? If you were going to change your display every six weeks to two months, what themes could you incorporate to make this effective?

TASK

Research how other therapists are using their display areas. Visit three therapists in your local area and notice the difference between the ways their services and products are displayed. Pay particular attention to professional environments. What do you like and dislike about the display area? What could be done better? What did you notice first about the display area?

TASK

Plan a changing display area taking the nature of your intended work space, waiting area and clients' interests into account. If you have more than one client group in mind, what special considerations would you make to cater to the interests of the different groups?

Expert Witness: **Working with the Media**

Andrew James practises reflexology, homeopathy, aromatherapy and massage. Having worked in the complementary therapies business for over 15 years, he also runs the Practitioner's School of Reflexology in west London and is the author of two books on Reflexology and Homeopathy. Andrew has had extensive experience working with the media and has frequently appeared on television and on the radio to promote the public's understanding of complementary therapies in general and his own practice as well.

Andrew knew that he wanted to be involved in training and promoting his subjects at an early point in his career, when he first got involved in helping other teachers set up courses or assisting in their teaching. He found that in making himself available to help he learned far more about the subject, including how much he had missed in the class. This willingness to help paid dividends, as he was then offered a job at the school where he trained as an assistant to the main tutors. This built up to taking classes in the tutors' absence and was a very interesting process,

" *I learned a lot from my teaching peers, mainly through questioning and listening to the way they delivered their lessons. It was at this time that I realised that you can't just do a course and think that you learn everything there is to know about it. Learning about therapies is a continual process, I'm still learning new things today.* **"**

continued...

I started teaching introductory courses to promote myself and my clinics, mainly doing day workshops on a very basic level as I found that I picked up a lot of clients this way. They would learn a few skills in the process, meet me in my capacity as a practitioner and would often come for treatment afterwards or recommend my services to friends and family members. This got me the connections I needed to move into the media side of things. I think that running workshops or free talks of this nature is absolutely essential if you do want to go into TV and radio work, as you get the practice you need at standing up, speaking effectively and confidently and thinking on your feet.

I first became interested in media work when I set up some new introductory courses at the adult college in Richmond. This got quite a lot of interest from the local press as it was the first time classes of this nature were available at the college. They were invited along to the classes and, although they didn't always show up, occasionally a feature article or write up would appear, in which they would usually mention my private practice as well.

The other thing I did was to contact local journalists and offer a free treatment. This worked best when it was relating to a health-related theme and gave me a chance to explain what the therapy was and how it works. I was very lucky with this approach, as I got some great publicity in the process, including one article where the journalist said they came away from the treatment 'walking on air' – that was great for me, and generated lots of interest.

continued...

After that I started writing articles for bigger, national publications, such as *Here's Health, the* Sun *and the* Sunday Times. *It was at this point that doors really started to open. I found myself treating people involved with the media and TV and started working for various radio stations, doing regular hour-long slots that featured health phone-ins and topical subject matter. Once I'd done a bit of the media work, I realised that I quite enjoyed it and that I was also good at it. At this point I was approached by the Learning Channel, which led to some TV work, including a range of programmes on stress for Cable 17 and some work with GMTV as well.*

If you are wanting to work with the media, the best advice I can give you is to

○ *know your subject matter and make sure you are completely confident with it*

○ *warm up to it – get involved at a local level first, before you move to national TV and radio. Allow yourself to grow and learn from the process, local residents are usually a bit more understanding of you if you make mistakes in the way you present yourself initially as you are one of their own*

○ *be prepared – get your friends to test you by asking different questions. This is especially important if you are planning to work in radio. Try and work out how long it took you to answer and whether it sounded confident, sympathetic and sensible*

continued...

○ *stay within your personal limitations – opportunities will arise, but only take them when you are ready for them and feeling confident. Work at your own pace and the confidence will grow steadily. Remember that when you are in such a public position it is better not to do something than to do it badly. If you are offered the choice, go for radio before trying TV. With radio, no one can see you, so if you dry up or lose confidence, you could have some books with you as prompts to help you through the worst of it*

○ *get a website – this is highly recommended if you are involved in research, media promotion and if you are getting a lot of coverage. It allows people to respond immediately on seeing your publicity and can move them swiftly towards making the decision to try a treatment*

○ *maintain your efforts – once you have started to build up in your practice and in your work with the media, you must maintain your enthusiasm and efforts. Give yourself challenges which are attainable and which will help you to grow as a practitioner*

○ *don't neglect your practice for the public eye – remember that you are doing the media work in order to support your business and attract attention for it. Keep developing your practical knowledge and experience, as your business practice is only as good as your treatment. Anyone can learn a treatment routine, but it's when you excel at it that you become able to make each treatment unique for the client. That helps them feel special and cared for and brings them back*

continued...

Your work with the media cannot stand alone, your other marketing efforts must help to support it and to generate the results you want. Be sensible with your budget and don't blow it all at once; don't get talked into things by marketing people! Whatever marketing work you do must generate the results that you need. It is important to bear in mind that once you have done one advert, every other newspaper or magazine will ring you to try and get you to advertise in their publication too. Find out what works for you and stick to it!

What worked for me was practising in lots of different ways – through health clubs and clinics, providing a consultancy service for large companies giving lectures and workshops for staff on subjects like stress and health in general. I also worked through GP practices and national support groups and societies related to conditions like asthma, eczema, cancer, and Hodgkin's disease doing talks and demonstrations to explain how the different therapies might help.

Sometimes I would hire a hall, put on tea or coffee and offer an evening of lectures and demonstrations. These were often so successful I found myself turning people away. If you do something like this, promote the events via advertisements in the local papers. If the event is free, sometimes the paper will put the advert in free as well. The same is true of the magazines that specialise in health and complementary therapies; they usually have a diary section which lists events – a free mention is possible here rather than having to place a display advert.

continued...

" *The last two things to mention are that the only time success comes before work is in the dictionary. None of this can be done without perseverance and effort. Yet it is just as important to care for the carer; take time out for yourself, have regular treatments (even if this means trading treatments with a colleague), set up and maintain your personal support network as well. Just because you are completely involved in your business doesn't mean family and friends are. Keep a healthy balance to your interests and take time to connect with other people for the sake of the relationship, not just because you want to get something out of them (or they want to get something out of you).* "

Checking your understanding

1. What equipment would you expect to find in your workspace?

2. What local authority guidelines exist that affect the way in that you can practise?

3. What access requirements are necessary in your workspace in order to cater for your preferred client group(s)?

4. When might you be exempt from the need to have a local authority's licence to practise?

5. What steps can you take to control environmental pollution in your workspace?

6. How can you effectively manage interruptions to your work?

7. List the benefits to your business of an effective use of display areas.

8. What steps can you take to make a display effective?

9. Draw up a display plan outlining the range of displays you are going to build over the first year of your business. Your plan should include the themes you intend to develop, the products or services each theme will highlight and any equipment or materials you will need to dress the display area.

10. Design a display that features your products and services and highlights their effectiveness in the following

    (a) Supporting weight loss or gain

    (b) Increasing fitness levels

    (c) Improving flexibility

    (d) Supporting the immune system (against the common cold).

Developing your business idea **3**

Objectives

At the end of this chapter you should be able to

○ Define SWOT analysis

○ Identify your own strengths and weaknesses

○ Produce a SWOT analysis for your business

○ Work out how to turn your initial ideas into an action plan for the future development of your business

○ Define 'niche' market

○ Outline your business vision

○ Analyse the skills you have or want and how you might use them differently

○ Define 'unique selling point' (sometimes called 'unique selling proposition')

○ Identify your own 'unique selling points'

Introduction

More and more people are training in beauty and complementary therapies every day. If you combine the number of hairdressing, beauty and therapy centres, they outnumber every other kind of business on the high street.

This means is that there growing competition for clients as more therapists become available and may be willing to work for less than you are charging. It also means that you will need to use all your skills and experiences to make your fledgling business work. Finally, it does mean that the most successful therapist businesses can depend on using the skills or contacts you have made in other employment or in your personal life to bolster the initial success of your business.

Downshifting: this is a term used to describe the process of leaving full-time, usually highly demanding jobs, in order to get a less stressful way of living and to have more time for other priorities; as you would shift down through the gears when driving in order to slow the car down. This less stressful life could include moving away from a city, changing jobs to something less demanding (and usually involving a smaller income), moving into part-time work or self-employment.

Carrying out a skills analysis can help you to look at what you do now in a different way. As you complete the task below, think about the people you know or meet in the course of using your skills. Which groups of people do you enjoy working with most? Are they part of your plans for your business?

Skills Analysis

Identify all the skills that you currently have. Be as specific as you can be. Remember that things which you take for granted might be essential skills for the success of your business, or they could be skills that you could continue to use elsewhere whilst your business is growing but still not able to support you fully.

Question 1: What skills do you have now that are useful to the business you intend to set up?

Question 2: What skills would you be willing to use now to give you additional income if the business is slow to start?

Question 3: What skills do you have now that you really don't enjoy using and that you would really like to take a break from?

Question 4: What skills do you need to make the business run as you want it to? Do you need to learn these skills yourself, or could you get someone else to provide them for you?

FOR DISCUSSION

Are you a portfolio worker? Could you earn a living by combining several of your existing skills in a new way?

DEFINITION

Portfolio working/portfolio worker: this is a term sometimes used to describe people who do more than one kind of job at the same time. For example, they might practise as a therapist, work in a nursery school and teach swimming.

FOR REFLECTION
REFLECTION

Even the skills and experiences you don't enjoy or don't want to repeat can be useful in helping you work out how you want your business to develop. Think about why you don't like them – this can help you to be more specific about developing a situation where the work you do builds on the skills you enjoy using in an environment you like.

What kind of business vision do you have?

Every business starts with an idea or 'business vision'. One thing that makes a big difference between a successful business and a business that struggles and possibly sinks is the amount of time you spend refining those ideas and working out exactly what you want from your business and what you are able to give back to it. There is an ancient Chinese proverb that says 'be careful what you ask for, as you may get it' – this is the point at which you need to take time to work out exactly what you want from your business in order to make working an enjoyable experience.

A business vision that is going to work will do one or more of the following:

Figure 3.1 What is your business vision?

- ○ allows you to practise all the skills that you enjoy doing
- ○ lets you do this in an environment that you enjoy and that also meets your ideal client's needs and expectations
- ○ lets you work with people or groups of people you like
- ○ lets you work the amount you like, at the time you like and that also meets your client's needs and expectations
- ○ gives you the income that you want to achieve with respect to the business.

In order to work out your business vision, try answering the following questions:

- ○ identify a gap in the market that you can fill (and that you are willing to fill)
- ○ provide a way of making things better, easier or more fulfilling for your clients
- ○ identify a group of clients who need some product or service (which you can provide) and which they currently have no or limited access to
- ○ suggest a way of providing a service (such as treatments) or products that makes getting this service more attractive to the clients you have identified.

A business vision that is special to you should be one that also

- ○ excites you because it is special and different
- ○ makes you want to talk about it to everyone (you will be doing your marketing at the same time!)

Who	do you want to treat?
What	are they currently missing by not having treatments from you – is this different from what other practitioners are offering them?
Where	are you going to practise, is this significantly different from what other therapists are providing?
When	are you going to be practising (daytime/night-time/weekends) – is this a key issue for your clients?
Why	is your service going to be more appealing to your clients?
How	much are you going to charge them for your services? Will they be willing to pay this for what you are offering?

For Example

Ian has just finished training as a sports massage therapist and needs help deciding what his business vision should be. He knows he wants to be a good and effective therapist and to be open to treating anyone who wants a treatment (as he needs to make a good living from this work). When he started working from home and sent out his leaflet, he was surprised that no one seemed to be interested in having treatments. Carol helped him to work out his business vision by taking him through the questions above and concentrating on his existing skills and interests. Within a few minutes, Ian's problems were resolved and he knew what his next steps were going to be in terms of beginning to market himself effectively. He also realised that he had to change where he was working, when he was working and how he was promoting himself in order to make his vision work for him.

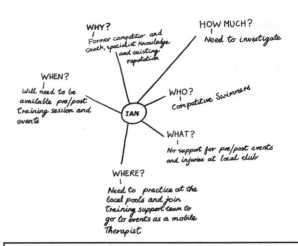

WHY?
Former competitor and coach, specialist knowledge and existing reputation

HOW MUCH?
Need to investigate

WHEN?
Will need to be available pre/post training session and events

WHO?
Competitive Swimmers

WHAT?
No support for pre/post events and injuries at local club

WHERE?
Need to practice at the local pools and join training support team to go to events as a mobile Therapist

Figure 3.2 Ian's expertise and interests lie specifically in working with amateur and professional swimmers

Draw up your own business vision. Be as specific as possible, especially when answering the questions above. Remember, even if you want to work with everyone in your local area, a business vision would concentrate on working out what makes what you do special and different from every other therapist in the area.

TASK

DEFINITION

business vision – *this is the term used to describe the idea or series of ideas that describes what you aim to do with your business. It will often be reflected in the business mission statement (see page 70) and business objectives but is usually a more general statement of your intentions.*

DEFINITION

'gap in the market' – *this term means that there is some product or some service that is not currently being provided. It could mean that the product doesn't exist yet or that what is available is not provided in the way that your ideal clients want it to be.*

DEFINITION

'niche market' – *a niche market is a very specialised portion of your target market (see page 78) that will need specialised treatment or special skills or experiences on the part of the therapist working with this group. If your target market was 'pregnant women who want Reflexology treatment' an example of a niche market might include 'pregnant women wanting Reflexology who are experiencing complications in the pregnancy'.*

The SWOT analysis

Once you have identified what your business vision is, the next step you need to take is to produce a SWOT analysis. Filling one in means that you have taken an objective look at yourself, your business, and your business environment in order to identify what is going to help you and what is going to make things difficult for you. Large businesses will often produce SWOT analyses at regular intervals as doing so makes you re-examine what you are doing and how, and can help you to improve your work as you are going along.

The objective in producing a SWOT analysis is to find ways of building on your strengths, minimising weaknesses, maximising opportunities and reducing threats. In practical terms, this may mean that your promotional literature will emphasise the areas that you are particularly good at (or interested in) working with and any relevant experiences you have (referring to your strengths).

The first two sections of a SWOT analysis – the strengths and weaknesses – concentrate on your internal environment; things going on within your business or, if you are a one-person business, these would refer to your personal strengths and weaknesses.

The second two sections – the opportunities and threats – concentrate on the external environment, or your market. Once you have your business vision, it is easier to identify possible opportunities for you to concentrate on. These could include relevant contacts you have who could help you find clients, outlets or venues who might be interested in letting you hold a talk or demonstration or who would like you to practise there, and so on. Threats refer to anything that could disrupt your plans. Often this can relate to the competition. As you fill in these sections, be as honest as you can be about the competition and what their strengths and weaknesses are as well. Remember that their weaknesses could become your opportunities as these weaknesses could indicate gaps in your market.

DEFINITION

SWOT analysis – this stands for 'Strengths, Weaknesses, Opportunities and Threats'.

For Example

Moira holds qualifications in Alexander technique, massage and sports massage. Her business vision involves helping dancers to recover faster from injuries and to improve their performance. Her SWOT analysis looks a little like this:

Strengths	Weaknesses
Qualified practitioner in AT, M and SM Experience teaching dance to amateurs (adults and children) 12 years' experience as a professional dancer AT can provide self-help techniques to speed recovery AT plus massage as diagnostic skillsto identify most useful stretchesor exercises for the individual	Haven't updated my teaching qualifications Out of touch with the professional dancing scene (but I know where to find out more)
Opportunities	Threats
There's a room to practise from in the local dance school Could run workshops on AT for dancers from local dance Could promote AT through library and local health centre and gyms Jane doesn't do AT, she works only on Thursdays and Fridays and only from the gym	Jane Smith down the road provides sports massage to dancers from the gym. She also charges less than I can afford to charge

DISCUSSION

What advice would you give to Moira? Can you think of any other opportunities that might be available to her? What about other potential threats? What do you think she should do about the one threat she has identified?

Fill in the SWOT analysis below for your business, thinking about your business vision. What are its strengths? Where are its weaknesses?

Strengths	Weaknesses
Opportunities	**Threats**

The unique selling points

Producing a SWOT analysis allows you to move on to develop a list of the unique selling points that you have to offer. These unique selling points should be things that you have identified from considering

- your strengths
- your opportunities
- the gap you have identified in the market (and how your service fills it better than anyone else's)
- your competitors' weaknesses (or how they are not meeting your clients' needs).

DEFINITION

The unique selling point, or USP, is the thing, or things; that makes your business significantly different from anything else available to your clients. These are the key reasons that your customers are going to come to you rather than anyone else.

In order to sell your services or products effectively, the unique selling points have to be

- something your clients strongly desire
- clearly spelled out in your promotional literature
- something you believe in and are prepared to talk about whenever you can
- something that is easy to explain or can be clearly experienced by the client.

To promote your business successfully, you need to be aware of what your unique selling points are: what is it about you and what you offer that is special? As Trevor points out (below), a lot of therapists don't look further than price when considering what may attract clients to them.

Expert Witness: Identifying your unique selling points

Trevor practises and teaches massage and karate. With over 20 years' experience in marketing and design, including running a highly successful marketing agency, he offers very clear advice to his students as they prepare to go out to work for themselves:

"

The people who will succeed in complementary therapies are the ones who would succeed in any other business and who aren't afraid to use what they learned elsewhere as they embark on a new career. To succeed, you need to have a tight control over what you do and who you are. You need to be sufficiently soft and receptive to give your clients the care and attention they desire, whilst being sufficiently firm to ensure you are paid appropriately for the service you offer. The last thing you want is to get to the end of the massage and have your client tell you they don't have any money or can't pay you what you are asking for.

I've noticed that new therapists tend to be afraid to charge the fee that they need to in order to cover their costs and still make a profit. They are more likely to price too low, without realising that the minute you go in as the cheapest therapist around, you have nothing else to give. Clients are aware of this and, whilst you will get the bargain hunters, a low price may not bring you the clients you want to attract or the respect and consideration your services deserve.

continued...

It's important to remember that you can have something cheap, you can have something quick, or you can have something good, but you can never have all three at the same time. New therapists in particular need to think very clearly about what makes their services different from those of every other therapist in their area. Price and location are not enough. „

Identify at least six unique selling points about your business. These should be things that are particularly important to the clients you wish to treat.

HINTS & TIPS

Remember that the care you provide, your experiences and the environment that you work in are part of the product available. You may find it useful to ask some of your existing clients or friends and family members about what they find special or different about the service you offer.

Your customer, your competitors and you

Your customer has a very special place in the relationship between you and your competitors; they will be making choices as to whose services they prefer and why. The customer goes through a clear process of making a decision to buy your services. Understanding that process can help you to make clear judgements about how, when and where to promote your work effectively.

Customer buying decision process

1. Recognises a problem exists
2. Finds out what is available to solve the problem
3. Makes a selection between the available alternatives
4. Buys the product or service
5. Decides whether they liked it and would go back again.

Consumer buying decision process – this identifies the five stages involved in deciding to buy a product or service: recognising the problem, finding information, choosing between alternatives, purchase of the product or service, and evaluating its effectiveness after purchase.

TASK

Effectively marketing your services involves helping the customer to move swiftly through this process and (hopefully) make them so impressed with you that they come back again soon. To do this consider how you fit into each stage of the decision process:

Recognising the problem

○ What problems are your target customers facing?

○ Are they aware of what symptoms you could help relieve?

○ Have you identified these symptoms on your promotional material?

○ If you are interested in working with particular conditions, are you in touch with the people who would help the customer to recognise the problem and then might put them in touch with you?

○ Is the information about the problem readily available to clients who might have it?

Finding information

○ Where would you turn to for information about this particular problem?

○ Are your services available in the places you identified as sources of information?

○ If they aren't available here, are your services promoted here?

continued ...

continued . . .

Making a selection

○ *What would make someone choose you? Are your unique selling points easily identified?*

○ *How can you make it easier for them to choose you?*

Buying the service

○ *Once they have made the decision to come to you, what can you do to make sure that the treatment is a satisfactory one for them?*

○ *What other elements of your service can you fine-tune to make the treatment extra special?*

Evaluating the outcome

○ *Do you ask your clients how they feel after the treatment?*

○ *What about checking how they are doing a couple of days later? Is this feasible for you?*

○ *What about a client evaluation form – so you can get feedback on your services, even if they decide not to come back? Do you think your clients would fill something like this in?*

Your competitors

What happens if a client asks you what the difference is between you and your competitor? With any luck, you will have found out what services your competitor offers and have an opinion as to how you compare. It may be that the person identified as your competitor offers a different form of treatment or practises in a different way. In these cases, you may have to explain the difference between the different kinds of therapy available. If the competitor identified practises exactly the same discipline as you do, you may wish to concentrate on describing your unique selling points.

Customer relationship management – this term is usually used to indicate ways in which you can use technology to improve your relationships with your clients or to improve sales. The purpose of this is to get more of your customer's purchases. For example, your suppliers might send you details of special offers by post or email to get you to buy products more often. They might also phone you with details of special offers if you don't respond to their post.

DISCUSSION

How could you use technology to improve your relations with your customers?

Fair play

Both you and your competitors are trying to attract the attention and interest of your customers and sometimes, if times are hard, the fight for clients could get fairly heated. At times such as this, remember that it is important to play fair, as not doing so can get you into trouble later along the line and could lose you clients in the long run. Playing fair, in this case means:

○ do not compare yourself to your competitors in promotional literature or in speaking – in severe cases this could be construed as libel

○ do not dismiss your competitor's work or efforts or cast doubts on their professional behaviour. You may find that one day your competitor becomes your colleague

○ concentrate on accentuating the positive aspects of what you do, this will bring positive work experiences towards you

○ if times are hard, revisit your business vision and SWOT analysis and see if anything has changed. Hard times can be an opportunity for you to change things and they may give you a chance to make things better than they have been before.

Competition oriented pricing – where you set your price based solely on what your competitors are charging, not considering your own costs or possible income. This usually means charging somewhat less than your competitors. Whilst you might get clients initially, if you haven't considered your costs in the long term, you may lose money rather than make it.

Competitive advantage – these are the things you do in order to give your business an advantage over your competitors and make your services or products more attractive to your clients. They usually relate to being less expensive, offering different benefits to the client or adding value to your services in another way. For instance, you might choose to provide small samples of products for home care as part of the treatment, as a means of adding value.

When competitors become colleagues

Whilst competitors are potentially striving for the same clients that you are, there is a very real possibility that you may work better together than apart. The benefits of working with someone who was a competitor or who practises in a similar discipline include

○ having someone to refer clients to – if you suspect the client would benefit from a different kind of approach or a different discipline

○ having more hours available to practise – you and your new colleague could provide a more comprehensive service to your clients, especially if you are both limited by other commitments to the number of hours you can work

○ reduced administration – share the load and it becomes more manageable and usually less costly

○ shared marketing costs – this means you might actually be able to improve the marketing you do, increasing the size or number of adverts, the quality of your marketing or even the number of outlets you are promoted in

○ shared strengths and increased opportunities – sharing your experiences can give you renewed interest and enthusiasm for your work and new ideas for getting things done

○ minimising weaknesses and threats – you may find that your colleague's strengths will balance your weaknesses and vice versa. Furthermore, if you are no longer a threat to each other, you may now be in a position to work more effectively and increase the number of clients you are getting

○ someone to cover your clients for you when you are ill or on holiday.

Developing a business relationship of this kind needs to be of benefit to both parties as well as providing a significant improvement in the service available to your clients. You also need to make sure that the person or persons you have identified are people whom you feel confident and happy working with and where there are shared experiences and shared goals. As a group, the new business partners would need to spend some time working out whether they share the same business vision – of what they want to do, and the same objectives – as to how they are going to get there.

Case study: The unexpected threat

Sandra practices Indian head massage and rents a treatment room in two centres. She noticed that she was suddenly losing clients at one of the centres after one of her colleagues added head massage to their qualifications. She initially assumed that this was a passing phase as it was a traditionally slow time of the year for her, until she noticed that virtually all of her clients were disappearing or failing to book further appointments. This was followed up by a visit from a long-term regular who led Sandra to discover that her newly qualified colleague had been offering treatments at a price lower than Sandra did, that she had got access to Sandra's clients' telephone numbers from the receptionist's bookings diary, had contacted them specifically about her new service and suggested that Sandra's treatments were out-of-date and possibly dangerous. The receptionist had also been encouraged by the therapist to refer all requests for Indian head treatments to the newly qualified therapist.

Sandra took the issue up with the manager of the centre, who was unaware of what was going on. The newly qualified therapist lost her position in the centre in question, as did the receptionist who had given her unauthorised access to client details. The manager also wrote to all of Sandra's clients expressing confidence in her services, experience and professionalism. Although some of her former clients did begin to return to her, not all did. Based on her experiences, Sandra made a few decisions:

continued ...

continued ...

○ to improve relations with her other colleagues practising other disciplines in both centres (and through the local community) so that this kind of event wouldn't happen again

○ to improve relations with the receptionists in the places that she worked in as they could seriously affect her success as a therapist

○ to improve her reputation as an effective and professional therapist after the damage that had been done

○ to change some aspects of the way she works and finds clients so that she is less vulnerable to unprofessional behaviour from her competitors.

Question: What could Sandra do to improve relations with other colleagues and with the receptionists?

Question: What could Sandra do to improve her reputation as a therapist, bearing in mind that she has been working for some time?

Question: What changes to her work could Sandra make? Would any of these things help to make her less vulnerable to others' behaviour?

Question: How could the newly qualified therapist have promoted her services more effectively and in a professional manner without risking her job or upsetting Sandra?

Question: What rules do you think should be in place in a treatment centre to protect the interests and business of the individual therapists like Sandra? What about the interests and business of the centre, should the therapist try to leave and take clients with them?

DEFINITION

Crisis management – this is the action or series of actions you take when a disaster happens. In marketing terms, this usually relates to the appearance of negative publicity. In a crisis, the therapist needs to respond quickly with appropriate publicity, explain the facts accurately and in full detail and be available should additional explanations be required.

FOR DISCUSSION

Can you identify what the unique selling points are of your main competitors? Do you share any of these USPs? If yes, you could add them to the 'Strengths' section of your SWOT analysis. If no, add them to the 'weaknesses' side of your SWOT analysis, but only if you think they are significant.

Checking your understanding

1. What is meant by a skills analysis?
2. What is a business vision? How can having one help your business to succeed?
3. Explain niche marketing, how is it different from target marketing?
4. What is a SWOT analysis?
5. What is a unique selling point?
6. What are the stages of the consumer-buying decision process?

7. What steps do you take to make sure your clients find it easy to buy your products or services?
8. What is the purpose of getting your customers to evaluate your service to them?
9. What is customer relationship management? How can you use it with your clients?
10. What is meant by a competitive advantage?

At the end of this chapter you should be able to

○ Explain what is meant by a product-led, a sales-led and a market-led business

○ Explain how and when each of these styles of business would be appropriate

○ Analyse your potential client's needs

○ Explain what is meant by a PEST Analysis

○ Produce a PEST Analysis for your business and clients

○ Explain how knowing what your clients need will help increase your ability to sell products and services to them

Introduction

Knowing who your clients are, what they want and how to reach them is one of the keys to success. However, this is one aspect that a lot of therapists can overlook; we spend a lot of time perfecting our treatments – the product/service we are selling, and the process of the treatment – without thinking about who we want to sell to and whether what we are selling is what that person wants.

Once you have identified your clients, your next step will be to establish a rapport with them, through your marketing and promotional activities, so that they know that you understand them and their needs and that you are able to meet those needs.

Figure 4.1 Selling your business

DEFINITION

Marketing involves identifying your clients' needs, satisfying them and making a profit.

Product-led, sales-led or market-led?

Businesses tend to fall into one of these three categories depending on the focus of the company and the emphasis it places on different aspects of their business.

A product-led company is one that focuses on the products they sell, sometimes to the exclusion of all other aspects. They will spend a lot of time and energy on developing new products and, although it is not always said, there is sometimes a belief that improving the product is the most important thing they can do. 'Build a better mouse-trap, and the world will beat a path to your door.' The pricing of the product is more likely to reflect the cost of developing it than it is to reflect what clients are likely to pay for it. Promotion is more likely to highlight the features of the product or service.

A sales-led company is going to be more interested in the number of products they sell. Sometimes they will make cuts on quality in order to sell more products. Some sales-led companies will focus on selling something to each client and will argue that the sale is more important than making sure that the product is right for the client. Pricing will often reflect whatever action is required to make the most sales. Look for discounts for buying in bulk or when clients are strongly urged to book a set of treatments and pay in advance.

A market-led company will focus on their clients and make sure that the product or service they provide is appropriate to the client, meets their needs and even anticipates the needs (before the client is aware of needing something). Promotion will identify the benefits to the client. Pricing will be based on research carried out to work out what is acceptable to the client and the therapist.

Generally businesses are encouraged to be market-led. If you know what your customers need and want, you will not only be prepared to supply it, but you will also develop a habit of listening to your clients so that you can anticipate change when it occurs and plan for your business to react to those changes and therefore survive in a very competitive world. With this comes the potential to make the most profit – your customers are happy as their needs are met and will return for more, bringing their friends with them.

As therapists, our businesses can span all three categories. For instance, a product-led business might be one in which you focus solely on the product or service you are offering. Perhaps you spend a lot of time engaging in updating your skills or developing new skills, perhaps you have set your price for a treatment without looking to see what other therapists are charging around you. You may have decided that the product or treatment you offer is more effective than what others are offering and that you have priced it accordingly and promoted it as such. Whilst this approach can be dangerous if there is a lot of competition and people aren't aware of the things that make your treatment unique, a product-led approach can be necessary where you are the first person in the area to supply a particular product or service and where you are, therefore, required to educate your potential clients about your service prior to selling it to them.

A sales-led therapy business might involve concentrating on the number of treatments you can carry out in a day, focussing on filling up all available treatment slots, even if it means working at a discount, ensuring that each client that you treat is also encouraged to take away at least one product (which you also sell), and that your promotional literature and contact with the client concentrates on regular, frequent treatments. A sales-led approach, which can sometimes be seen as pushy or unconcerned with the needs of the client (focussing instead on the financial gains made by the therapists), can be an appropriate stance to take as a business starts up. Whilst you are introducing your new business to your clients, increasing the number of treatments you provide, and ensuring that you see a large number of different clients, are going to be beneficial in the long run to the success of your business.

The key difference between a sales-led and a market-led business, even in the launch phase of the business, will be the way in which the therapist focusses on his/her clients and how they try to attract their clients. The sales-led therapist will be trying to attract everyone, no matter where they come from. The market-led therapist will have taken the decision to concentrate his/her promotional activities on attracting the clients that they want to deal with and ensuring that their promotional literature reflects those clients' needs and desires and appears in the places where their desired clients would see them. A market-led therapist would still be able to carry out a very busy and active promotional campaign as the business starts up, but look for a more specialised slant to their leaflets, not a general leaflet outlining how their chosen treatment works.

FOR DISCUSSION

A lot of therapists choose to produce a leaflet that provides a general outline of what their therapy does, how it works, what to expect from a treatment and price details. Which category could you put these leaflets into – product-, sales- or market-led? Do you think leaflets of this nature work for every client? If yes, why? If no, then which clients does it work for and how would you change the leaflet to make it suitable for other groups?

DEFINITION

A feature is something that a product or service has. A benefit is something that it offers to the receiver. For example, a skirt could have a button, a zip and a slit at the back. These are all features. The benefits that these offer to the wearer are comfort and ease when putting on the skirt, more flexibility on walking, and (potentially) a more tailored appearance.

What is it your clients want?

An industrial psychologist, Maslow, developed a way of looking at how people's behaviour changed according to what they felt was most important to them at that time; what they wanted or needed. His hierarchy of needs looks like this:

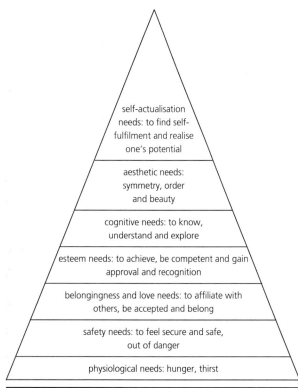

self-actualisation needs: to find self-fulfilment and realise one's potential

aesthetic needs: symmetry, order and beauty

cognitive needs: to know, understand and explore

esteem needs: to achieve, be competent and gain approval and recognition

belongingness and love needs: to affiliate with others, be accepted and belong

safety needs: to feel secure and safe, out of danger

physiological needs: hunger, thirst

Figure 4.2 Maslow's hierarchy of needs

Maslow argued that, unless basic physiological needs were met, people would not be interested in participating in activities that involved other factors further up the pyramid. Clients worrying about whether they have enough money to buy dinner for their family are not going to be thinking about paying for a treatment. However, if you are able to identify where your prospective clients are in Maslow's hierarchy of needs, and therefore what is most important to them at that time, you will be able

to communicate more effectively with them not only on a one-to-one basis when they come for treatment, but you will be able to include references to what you perceive as their needs in your promotional material. Furthermore, different groups of clients will have different needs, and identifying their needs helps you make a more profound connection with them and helps to build a rapport with your client from the moment they see your promotional material – long before they walk in the door for treatment.

For example

Steve practises massage, on-site massage, sports massage and nutrition and is also a personal trainer. He identified three distinct groups of clients that he wanted to work with: professional athletes, recovering addicts, and over-stressed business executives. On examining Maslow's hierarchy of needs, he decided that

○ The professional athletes were interested in performance or self-actualisation, so he should include details about how his services improved performance in all promotional literature aimed at them and home-care advice should also centre around these ideas.

○ The recovering addicts were concentrating on their physiological needs – most particularly for the substance or habit they were trying to break, so that the promotional literature aimed at them should feature the effectiveness of his work in reducing cravings and supporting the recovery process.

○ The over-stressed business executives Steve felt less sure about. He felt there were some security issues (some of the clients were afraid of losing their jobs), there were some social issues (people worrying about bullying in the workplace and feeling that they were trading-off work and home commitments and handling both badly) and there were also some ego issues (the desire to perform more efficiently and effectively, and be recognised for it). His response with these groups was to carry out market research by interviewing someone in the human resources department of each of the large companies who invited him in to provide on-site services, in order to find out what they had identified as key issues within their own staff. He then found himself producing different posters to promote his services at each company, based on what the human resources department had identified. He also changed the posters regularly in order to see how interest in his business also varied.

TASK

Consider each of the client groups listed below, paying particular attention to any that you feel you would like to work with (or add them to the list). What do you think are their key needs? What do you think would make them want to try your services?

- ○ *Amateur athletes*
- ○ *Couples receiving infertility treatment*
- ○ *Other therapists*
- ○ *Pregnant women*
- ○ *Those recovering from ME*
- ○ *Cancer patients*
- ○ *Those with Repetitive Strain Injury*
- ○ *Those with Irritable Bowel Syndrome*
- ○ *Families and carers of Alzheimer's patients*

Successful selling

The key to selling products or services is to understand your client's needs, express that understanding to the client and give them the reasons they need to hear to help them decide to buy what you are selling them. To do this effectively, you do not need to push too hard, in fact many clients will feel suspicious if you place too much emphasis on product sales and may find themselves wondering if your intentions are genuinely to look after their interests or simply to get a commission.

As a result, there is a fine line to walk when you are involved in selling products: don't push too hard, but give the clients what they need to help them make a decision if they are interested. Remember that nothing will get sold unless the client knows about the products and is aware of what benefits these products could offer them. Successful selling involves taking the following steps in order:

- ○ ask the client what they want – be as precise as you can in your questioning

- ○ identify what the client's logical and emotional responses to your product or service are

- ○ explain the benefits of the product or service in terms of how it matches these logical and emotional responses

- ○ clarify with them that you have given them the information they need. Check if they need any other information

- ○ ask for their decision – would they like to book now/buy the product(s) in question? (Try not to offer the opportunity to think it over. They will

take that option if they need it anyway, but if they are on the edge of making the decision, this will usually encourage them to take the plunge immediately.)

'Just looking'

A favourite phrase when you are out shopping, we have all used this one at times, and it is generally very effective at getting rid of sales staff. However, if you are being encouraged to sell products or services and want to be more effective, try changing the wording of your questions, making them more open-ended. For example:

Before	After
Can I help you?	How may I help you? (It's very difficult for people to say 'leave me alone!' to this)
Have you considered trying a complementary treatment?	What would you like to get out of a treatment? or What benefits are you hoping to gain from a treatment?

DISCUSSION

What other phrases do you find yourself using if you are trying to interest a client in buying a product for homecare? How could you change those sentences to encourage the client to talk about what they want?

Logic vs emotion

Each person makes their decisions to buy anything by considering logical, practical reasons AND emotional, personal reasons. A successful sales person will be able to identify what the client's reasons are on both

levels. All that is required is that you listen to what the client says and ask more questions.

For example:

Bethany works as a massage therapist within a salon environment. Whilst covering reception one day, she got chatting to a new client who knew nothing about the products they had for sale, but wanted to buy a present for a friend and had a very limited time in which to make a decision. On further questioning, Bethany worked out that this client was going to make a decision based on the following factors:

Logical	Emotional
Limited time to spend on decision Reasonable budget	Gift must look beautiful and expensive (but not be so) Gift needs to look as if much effort and thought went into its choice Friend in question is very particular about cosmetic products and very knowledgeable Friend has very sensitive, dry skin

As a result, Bethany pointed the client in the direction of the latest additions to the range, and outlined their key benefits in terms of their effects on the skin. The client quickly picked out a gift set that she liked and had made her purchase within ten minutes of starting the conversation.

It is also very important to recognise that the emotional level is usually far more powerful during a decision-making exercise. Appealing to the client on an emotional level will often get the desired results. This is why therapists are not allowed to say that they are able to 'cure' anything; a potential 'cure' is an extremely powerful message, especially in the hands of someone who is less than ethical.

DEFINITION

Open-ended questions are ones that require a full answer. A close-ended question can be answered with one or two words, usually 'yes' or 'no'.

Closing the sale

Four out of five people wait to be asked if they want to book a treatment or take a product. If you have worries about your ability to sell products or treatments, the tendency is to forget to ask the final question and get the booking or sell the product. It is very important for the success of your business (or that of your employer) that you overcome any fears in this area. Asking the client if they are interested in booking a treatment is not a pushy thing to do, especially if they have just been asking you about your work and the benefits of a treatment!

Using the following closing questions as examples, develop questions that you feel comfortable using and which will help you close your sales:

'Would you like to buy that (product) then?'

'Does this treatment sound like one that would benefit you/that you would enjoy?'

TASK

What do you assume your clients want?

Draw up a list of all the reasons your clients might have for buying a treatment from you (or not). Do this without asking your clients for any suggestions, then compare your answers with the details you get from carrying out the market research exercise later in this chapter. A couple of suggestions have been included in the table below to help get you started:

To buy	Or not to buy
Price as expected	Price (too high or too low)
Convenient location	Travel time is inconvenient
Easy to get a booking	Difficult to get an appointment
Added value (but what?)	

DISCUSSION

Look at the list of 'reasons not to buy' produced above. If your prospective clients said these were a problem, how would you handle the situation? Can you turn their objections around so they see them in a positive light, or do the objections they raise indicate serious problems with your business?

Market research

Evidence of market research to support your business vision, and to inform your marketing, is a requirement for most business plans, because doing the right kind of research can help you to find out what your clients want, what your competitors are doing and to work out how best to sell your services.

There are a number of ways you can carry out market research – from interviewing people for their opinions and advice, to producing questionnaires for them to fill in, to collecting all the leaflets available about the treatments offered by your competitors. The way in which you carry out the research depends on which questions you want answered and how you want them answered. Some of the reasons you might conduct market research include the following:

- To find out what your competitors offer (including their unique selling points)

- To find out what prices people are charging or expect to be charged

- How many therapists are practising locally

- Where do they practise? What days, times, hours?

- To find out what magazines, newspapers, journals, or similar are read by your preferred clients

- To find out what local services are used by your preferred clients

- To find out when your clients would use those services and when (time of day and year) they might want to use your services

- To discover what influences your preferred clients to buy/not to buy treatments

- To discover what benefits and features your preferred clients will look for in a treatment.

DISCUSSION

What other reasons can you think of to carry out market research?

Once you have decided to carry out market research, there are a few issues to consider if you are trying to get information out of your preferred client groups and this information will influence how you set up and promote your business. Try to ensure that you

○ interview a large number of potential clients (so you have a more objective view)

○ give them opportunities to say what they think, rather than leading them to a limited choice of answers. This can give you some very enlightening ideas about how to progress with your business

○ make sure the people you interview are typical of your preferred clients so that the answers they give are likely to reflect those of the whole group

○ plan the questions you are going to ask in advance, so that you are prepared for what you need to ask

○ consider how you will record information; if you write slowly, you may wish respondents to fill in a form or to tape record them speaking

○ give an incentive – if you give people a questionnaire to take away and fill in, they will need a reason to fill it in and return it. Consider what you might offer in advance – possibly a chance to win a free treatment or product?

TASK

Carrying out market research. Each of the steps outlined here is designed to help you get as clear a picture as possible of your clients (and their needs) plus your competitors (and how, if at all, they are meeting your clients' needs).

(1) *Your competitors – Who are they? What do they offer? How much do they charge? When are treatments available? Where are they working? What are their unique selling points? Try to be as detailed as possible and include all the competitors you can find within a 20–30 minute travelling time of the venue you want to work from. (If you believe people will travel for longer in order to get a treatment, then expand your working area.) Possible sources of information will include any leaflets you can find as well as Yellow Pages advertisements, information provided by governing bodies for the different therapies, local shops, health centres, and similar.*

continued ...

TASK

② *Your clients – what do they want from a treatment? Do they want treatments generally? What are their expectations of a treatment? How much would they pay for a treatment; how often do they want treatments; how do they want to hear about therapists; where might they expect to get further information; if they currently receive treatments, are they satisfied with them? What improvements could be made? Produce this list as a questionnaire, which potential clients can fill out and hand back. The easiest and least time-consuming questionnaires (which have multiple choice answers provided) are the fastest ones to do, so you may find you get more responses if you produce these. Aim to get at least 20 responses if possible.*

③ *Check your list of assumptions about their needs and the potential reasons you came up with as to why they might not want to buy a product. Check these now with potential clients to find out how important these issues are and whether your assumptions were correct. Try asking about what they want in an open-ended fashion, as it may be that something you thought was really important, perhaps keeping the price as low as possible, isn't as vital as you believed. These assumptions and needs will take longer to discuss. Do this part of the research as short interviews with your existing clients – they may feel they know you well enough to be direct and may feel honoured that you are asking for their advice and suggestions on how to improve your business.*

The PEST analysis

One of the most useful things that market research can tell you about your clients and potential clients is the factors that can influence their decision to buy a treatment. In chapter 7 we talk about some of the personal influences that can encourage a client to buy a treatment, things such as friends/family who have booked a treatment and got a lot of benefit out of the session, and so on. There are often other factors involved as well; things that don't seem immediately relevant at first but which could sway your client. Generally we divide these into four categories:

○ Political

○ Economic

○ Social

○ Technical/technological

For example, the events of September 11th 2001 affected small and large businesses around the world, not just those in the USA or the travel industry. People were afraid of what the events could mean for them and there was a tendency to spend less on anything that wasn't absolutely necessary for survival. Things like holidays, entertainment, treatments, buying a new house, car or luxury item were no longer as important.

The PEST Analysis contains things that are often outside your immediate influence but which could affect your client's decision to buy a treatment. These things can be small or large in nature and could have a limiting effect on the business.

For example, Nigel works as an Acupuncturist and wants to extend his business from his existing venue (a set of treatment rooms about a health food shop) and is particularly keen to start working with physically handicapped people and the elderly. He carried out extensive market research in his area, and produced the following PEST Analysis

continued ...

Political	Economic
Influence of relevant support associations required to highlight effectiveness and usefulness of treatment to key client groups.	Economic downturn would reduce amount of surplus money that could be used for treatments.
Landlord of treatment centre concerned with additional health and safety issues.	Clients facing high costs for support and equipment for everyday life, little surplus financial support anyway.
Possible changes to funding and legislation means that Nigel could investigate providing his services through the NHS.	Some insurance companies now recognising complementary therapies and payments are possible for certain conditions as a result.

Social	Technical/technological
Transport issues involved in getting to/from treatment venue didn't fit with Nigel's working hours (evenings only), clients needing to rely on others to help with transport.	No wheelchair access to venue.
	Narrow steep stairwell, difficult for blind and frail people to use.
Working hours didn't allow for clients to combine treatment with other social events, thereby minimising demands on carers or similar.	No waiting area supplied for clients.
Few clients in the preferred group who also lived in Nigel's area had experienced the treatment and/or were willing to try it, so word-of-mouth marketing looked questionable.	

FOR DISCUSSION

Can you think of any other issues that might influence Nigel's chosen client group?

Based on his PEST analysis and additional research carried out, Nigel decided that he might be targeting the wrong client group if he was determined to continue to work from this venue. He decided that, whilst he would still actively seek to work with these clients, it would be more appropriate to provide his services to them on a mobile basis, visiting homes, hospices and offering small group 'coffee morning' style workshops for them and to pursue the possibility of working with the medical establishment.

To build up his business from the health centre, he chose instead to concentrate on those with digestive difficulties, as a detailed interview with the owner of the health food centre and their staff revealed that the bulk of the clientele asking advice in the shop sought information and support in this area. Further questioning on Nigel's part showed that over half the people using the shop fell into this category; he had a keen market whom he could work with that he hadn't been fully aware of until that moment.

> **Draw up your own PEST analysis, using the market research you carried out into your clients' circumstances as a basis for completion. What does this now show you about the issues facing your clients?**

Checking your understanding

1. What is meant by a product-led company?
2. What is the difference between being sales-led and market-led?
3. What steps can you take to help you sell products more effectively?
4. When might you carry out market research?
5. What steps can you take to make sure your market research is useful?
6. What could you do to encourage people to participate in your market research?

7. List five potential sources of information about your competitors.
8. What does PEST stand for?
9. Define marketing.
10. What have you learned about your clients and your competitors from carrying out your research? Use specific examples from your own circumstances.

5 Drawing up your business plan

At the end of this chapter you should be able to

- Explain what is meant by an objective
- Set your own objectives for your business
- Develop a business mission statement
- Explain how this business mission fits with your business idea
- Explain what is meant by business 'tactics'
- Explain what is meant by the 'marketing mix'
- List the contents of a business plan
- Develop your own business plan

Introduction

A successful business relies on detailed planning; planning that takes all your resources, skills and abilities into account, that includes ideas for what you will achieve if you are successful and which also outlines your contingency plans – what you will do if it doesn't go as you foresee. Most businesses fail in the first two years as a result of poor (or non-existent) planning. This includes those who do make the effort to produce plans and then do not revisit their plans. Don't neglect the financial figures (advice and guidance on producing these is found in chapter 6). This gives you definite goals to mark your achievement and will convince anyone you are seeking to borrow money from that you mean business.

If you carry out the tasks in this chapter, taking your time to answer all the questions involved, you will have done the basic planning needed in order to:

- approach a bank should you need a loan or an overdraft facility

- work out how, where and when you will be working
- decide how much and what kind of marketing you will need
- budget for all costs involved in the business
- work out how much of a contingency fund you will need
- prioritise effectively, so that you become aware of what it is most important for you to start doing next.

Remember, the more comprehensive your answers, the more it will help you to clarify your ideas about how you want your business to work.

The business plan

A detailed business plan will include all of the following elements:

(a) a mission statement that outlines the nature of your business

(b) details of the formation of the business, whether it is a partnership, a limited company, charity or sole tradership

(c) details of those involved and their existing commitments

(d) the objectives for the business

(e) an outline of the market you intend to focus on

(f) a PEST Analysis, if you are seeking financial support, showing what factors would affect your customers' purchasing decisions

(g) details of the prevailing conditions in the market place. This is slightly different from the PEST Analysis and talks about what represents a 'normal' pattern of behaviour and sales for the market you are targeting

(h) details of the products or services you are offering and an explanation of why they will appeal to the clients you intend to attract

(i) a price list, plus an explanation of the pricing policy you intend to operate, including an indication of when (and if) your prices will vary

(j) a marketing plan, showing how you intend to reach your clients, with details of how much you intend to spend on marketing

(k) analysis of the competition – this should show that you have researched your market and identified your competition's strengths and weaknesses. This may indicate how and why you have chosen your prices and must explain why your clients are more likely to choose your services over those offered by your competitors

(l) a SWOT Analysis for your business – indicating your own strengths and weaknesses and showing how you intend to turn any threats into opportunities

(m) details of premises, plants and fittings – where you will work, what equipment you need and any additional work that needs to be done prior to your commencing trading

(n) financial forecasts for the first five years of business, with an explanation of how you see this developing

(o) if you have sources of finance in place or identified, these will need to be listed as well

(p) an explanation of how you intend to monitor your business, how often you will do so and (if you are asking for a loan) what you intend to do if the business is not as successful as you foresee.

The business mission

At the beginning of a business plan, you will usually find the mission statement – a general sentence that outlines the nature of the business, but which doesn't include your immediate objectives. Many businesses choose to make this sentence extremely general so that as their businesses expand or develop they can incorporate new aspects, products or services to their work. The mission statement could remain constant throughout the life of your business, even if everything else changes: it explains your intentions.

The format of a mission statement could look like this: 'To provide (goods and services – what kinds?) to (whom?)

Devise a mission statement for a complementary health centre that is opening up in your area. Remember to consider all the possible goods and services that they could offer (even if they don't initially do so).

DEFINITION

A mission statement is a general statement or paragraph that outlines the nature of the business. These statements are kept as broad as possible so that at a later date you could expand your business into other areas without altering your original intentions for the business.

Business formation

The business plan should include details of the date on which you began (or intend to begin) trading and the format that your business is going to take.

There are a number of different possibilities open to you when choosing the format of your business. Each has distinct advantages and disadvantages, some of which are outlined below.

Sole trader

This is the format that many small businesses (and most therapists) choose to take. A sole trader is responsible for all aspects of the business and will take on any business debts as personal debts if the business should run into trouble. They have a tax advantage over the other business formats in that they are only taxed once – on their earnings after expenses are deducted at the end of the financial year. One drawback to becoming a sole trader is that, should you choose to get a loan or take out a mortgage at a later date, the banks will need to see at least three years of accounts to ensure that you are a reasonable credit risk and that you will be able to pay back the monies that you are asking for. The temptation for many sole traders is to run their businesses in such a way that they are just breaking even in order to avoid paying large sums in tax. Whilst that may work in the short term, if your long-term goal is to get property, it is advisable to keep expenses to a minimum, maximise your profits and be taxed accordingly.

Limited company

A limited company is the preferred option for those who want to limit the financial risks they are taking. If the company were to run up huge debts or be declared bankrupt, being limited would put a ceiling on how much the shareholders and directors are liable for. If you have property or other assets and work in a discipline where clients might sue you; or if your partner or dependants don't feel secure with your career choices, you may want to consider this format. (Remember that your professional insurance should cover you in the event of being sued by a client). As the owner of a limited company, you will be taxed twice – firstly the company will be taxed, secondly you will pay income tax as an individual on a PAYE basis.

DEFINITION

PAYE stands for 'Pay as you earn'. A PAYE salary indicates that the sums received by the employee are net (or after) Income tax and National Insurance have been paid.

Partnership/equity partnership

Going into business with one or more other therapists can help to ease the financial, administrative and marketing burdens as well as attracting additional clients to your door. If you do go into partnership, this is best handled via a solicitor who can produce a legal document, the partnership agreement, which clearly states exactly what each partner has contributed to the arrangement (in terms of finance, skills, time or services), the nature of their ongoing involvement and what they can expect to get out of it should the business be sold or if the relationship between the partners breaks down in any way.

Although solicitors' fees can be daunting, remember that they have a great deal of experience in making sure that every possible angle is covered, including clauses should one or more of you need to break the agreement, under what circumstances a partner could be bought out, whether a partner could sell their interest in the company without the agreement of the other partners, and so on.

FOR DISCUSSION

What other elements do you think should be part of a partnership agreement?

Charity

A charity is a non-profit making organisation. Charities receive certain tax benefits, which can be advantageous, and their work is always geared towards the welfare and well-being of the client group they are providing for. Any sums they receive are on a donation basis, so those sums received above and beyond expenses cannot be kept but must be returned in some shape or form to the client group; all work carried out is for their benefit.

DISCUSSION

Which kind of business format is going to be most appropriate for your business? Why?

Directors, owners, managers and their present commitments

Your business plan should outline the details of the individuals involved in your business, their appropriateness for the job, relevant qualifications and experiences. You can include curriculum vitaes for those involved if you wish, although a short paragraph outlining their work-related history is just as appropriate.

Do not neglect to highlight the commitments of those involved. If they are heavily committed, you might not be able to have as much of their time as you want.

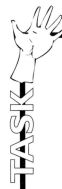

TASK

Using the work-related histories or curricula vitae of each member of your company, produce a list of unique selling points for the company. This might include the combined years of experience, the range of clients dealt with, and the variety of tasks that could be accomplished.

DISCUSSION

If time is limited, how would you ensure that you are using each of the key people in your company appropriately and to best effect? If you are planning to be a sole trader or work on your own, consider your existing support network. Who could you call on for help? What kind of help do you feel you need? Try to be as specific as possible.

REFLECTION

Do the individuals concerned have preferences in terms of the work they want to do? Is there any overlap – do people want to do the same task and are neglecting other, essential, tasks?

Individual preferences and the way your needs, wants and desires are met can be crucial to the success of the business. If all the members of your company are heavily committed but want to work together, not only because they enjoy each other's company but also because they are under the impression that 'someone else' is going to do the paperwork, get the clients and handle all bookings, you may run into problems sooner than anticipated. Make sure you consider carefully all the tasks that are going to be required, that you have discussed them and that everyone has the same understanding of how these tasks are going to be handled and by whom.

DISCUSSION

Are there other skills that are missing from the company? How are you going to address these gaps?

Identifying skills and experiences that are missing from your company can require a great deal of honesty. As we start up in business, we want to believe that we can accomplish anything and that we are equally good at (and willing to carry out) every aspect of what is required to make the business work. This is not always the case. However, identifying the problem will bring you one step closer to finding a creative solution to it. Creative solutions do not need to be expensive. Sometimes the answers can be very simple indeed. Consider some of the following:

○ Hate asking for fee – work in a centre with a receptionist/get a neighbour to be your receptionist.

○ Don't like filing your receipts – find someone willing to do your bookkeeping; your accountant may be able to recommend someone locally, or ask other therapists.

○ Marketing yourself feels dreadful – pay someone else to take your leaflets into various outlets (they may do this in exchange for a treatment).

○ Don't like mailing/packaging products – borrow the services of one of the neighbourhood kids to stuff envelopes and go to the post office.

○ Never get round to banking the takings – find someone you trust who is willing to make a regular trip to the bank on your behalf.

Objectives

In business terms, objectives are specific statements of intention that are

○ Manageable

○ Measurable

○ Achievable

Objectives tell the reader what you are trying to achieve. Aim to be as specific as possible. Include figures to indicate how much you want to turn over within set periods of time after setting up your business. Show that you expect the figures to grow over time and highlight the key areas of interest and key market areas you intend to work with.

Examples of objectives found in a business plan might include:

○ To provide (goods and services) to the community at large

○ To provide (goods and services) to the business/retired/infirm communities

○ To specialise in XXX

○ To create public awareness of the company

○ To carry out a minimum of XXX – treatments per week within six months of commencing trading

○ To achieve a turnover of £xxx,xxx (gross) within three years of commencing trading.

For example

Sarah is a highly qualified nutritionist with extensive teaching experience in nutrition and a strong interest in stress-related disorders, addictions and post-traumatic stress syndrome. She wants to build on her existing skills and experiences and provide a different kind of nutrition service and believes there is a great deal of room for improvement in the way other therapeutic disciplines provide nutritional advice. Some objectives that might be appropriate for her would include

○ To provide nutritional education and training services to the complementary and alternative practitioners nearby

○ To provide introductory level nutritional education and training to the general public by running courses and workshops at appropriate venues in the area

○ To specialise in supporting stress-related disorders and those withdrawing from addictive behaviour by working in conjunction with local counselling services, GPs and treatment centres

○ To create awareness of my services within these client groups via appropriate marketing

○ To carry out a minimum of four weekend workshops within six months of commencing trading

○ To achieve a turnover of £50,000 within three years of commencing trading.

DISCUSSION

If you consider Sarah's objectives, what would you expect to find in her marketing plan? Do you think her targets for turnover and the weekend workshops are realistic? What promotional items do you think would best meet her requirements?

DEFINITION

'Gross' or 'Gross Profit' usually refers to your profits before tax. 'Turnover' refers to your income before subtracting expenses.

Work out your personal and professional objectives

When you run a small business, remember that in many cases your personal objectives must run alongside the business ones or be clearly stated so that you and your business continue to work happily together. It is now time to ask yourself seriously what you want. Be as specific as possible. The following techniques may help you:

(a) Your 'I want' list

Picture yourself 10 years in the future. Using the following headings, write down what you want to have achieved within 10 years' time;

continued ...

TASK

continued ...

- ○ *Relationships*
- ○ *Family*
- ○ *Home*
- ○ *Hobbies/Interests*
- ○ *Travel*
- ○ *Work/Career*
- ○ *Creativity*
- ○ *Reputation*
- ○ *Personal development*
- ○ *Other*
- (b) *Using the same headings, indicate which goals you want to have achieved within 5 years' time*
- (c) *Using the same headings, indicate which goals you want to have achieved within 3 years' time*
- (d) *Using the same headings, indicate which goals you want to have achieved within 18 months.*

These four steps will have given you a number of objectives as well as a time span in which you want to achieve them. Transfer any business-related ones to your list of objectives above.

FOR REFLECTION

Some of the personal objectives you may have listed could have an impact on your business. How are they likely to do so? What do you need to do to ensure that you have the time and energy to carry out your business objectives and still have time to meet your personal objectives?

The Market

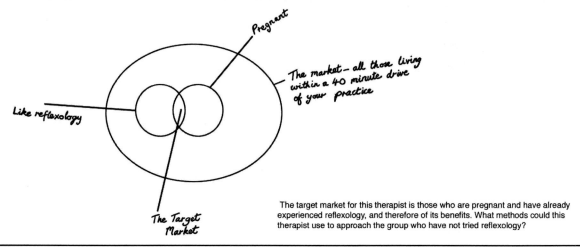

Pregnant

The market – all those living within a 40 minute drive of your practice

Like reflexology

The Target Market

The target market for this therapist is those who are pregnant and have already experienced reflexology, and therefore of its benefits. What methods could this therapist use to approach the group who have not tried reflexology?

Figure 5.1 Identifying your market

For your business plan you will need to include some details about the market you intend to work in. This section should indicate the groups of people you want to sell your services to and why they want to buy what you are selling. Marketing professionals will often tell you that targeted marketing, where you aim your services at a specific and identifiable group of people rather than at everyone in the local area, will usually get you a better response. You do not have to stick to one target market, but could have several whom you approach in slightly different, but specifically appropriate, ways.

DEFINITION

A target market sector is the specific part of a market that you are aiming your services at. For instance, 'the market' for your services might mean 'all people living within a 40-minute drive of where I work' – and indicate those catchment areas. Your 'target market' might mean 'all those living within a 40-minute drive who like reflexology and are also pregnant'.

An undifferentiated market approach – this assumes that all clients everywhere have similar needs and wants and can be appropriately serviced with exactly the same product they have seen before.

TASK

Produce a list of as many different target markets as you can think of. For your business plan, select the ones from your list that you are most interested in working with and write a brief description of these, which includes the following elements:

Why they would want or need your services or products

Why you want to work with them

Anything you know about when they are likely to want your services

How these target markets fit together – will they help to balance out slow and busy periods for you?

Note: You may wish to treat everyone! Yet each person is an individual with specific needs, wants and desires (see chapter 4). To attract them all you will need to approach them in different ways. It is easier and more cost effective to concentrate on certain groups first. Try putting the remainder of your list of target markets in the order of which groups you find most interesting to work with. This list can then form the basis of your ongoing marketing efforts as you begin to approach them at a later date.

Your explanation of the market should also include a brief outline of how you intend to sell your services to your target markets (this outline is then expanded on in your marketing plan – see chapter 7 for details), and the information you have that leads you to believe that they will buy from you.

For example

Anna's business plan showed that she intended to work with pregnant women within a 30-minute travelling distance of her venue (which was a treatment room behind a health food shop). In her section on 'The Market', she included information about dealing with local GPs, midwives, National Childbirth Trust groups and similar. She also pointed out that she would be including the fact that she was a former midwife in her promotional material along with the easy parking facilities and the location of the nearest bus stops. Anna intends to learn baby massage next so that she can add this service to her range and build on the business she intends to develop, so that her clients stay with her after their pregnancies are completed.

Helena Trump has a degree in Business Studies, a Chartered Institute of Marketing Diploma and has been practising as a complementary therapist for the past 10 years. She practises aromatherapy, reflexology, sports massage, diet and nutrition, counselling and psychotherapy. Aged 51, she has, throughout that time, been a single mother with three children, their expenses and a mortgage to cope with.

Helena first started her practice in a clinic in Taunton, the nearest large town, where she was based for four years before she had a full client list and decided to change to working from home, where the bills would be slightly lower.

" A lot of therapists and those who are considering practising complementary therapies forget what it can be like to be a single parent with no other source of income apart from what you bring in from therapy work. It can be lonely and it can be very tough, especially if you start to feel run down or you get sick. I do not have health insurance so if I don't work, I don't earn anything. Until recently I didn't realise that I could get sickness benefit because I paid my national insurance stamps. I was off for two weeks and, although you can't claim for the first few days, I was able to claim something, and that was a great deal of help. "

continued...

Helena feels that the key to making a success of a rural practice is professionalism in every aspect of your work. Each Sunday she spends three hours reading through her case notes for the clients visiting the forthcoming week, so that she is fully prepared when they arrive for treatment. She also pays very close attention to details: despite having several cats and dogs, the treatment room and the house do not smell of animals, she ensures the treatment room is warm and welcoming and that both the towels and the couch covers are changed for each client. Helena herself doesn't like the feel of couch roll, and prefers to pay the difference involved in the additional laundering of towels because it allows her clients to feel more pampered. At the start of each treatment, she reinforces the confidentiality of the treatment process, a feature she feels is particularly important in a rural practice when you are more than likely to run into half your clients in the high street on a regular basis. Furthermore, Helena makes sure that she takes time with her clients, allowing at least half an hour between sessions without fail so that she has the opportunity to straighten up all aspects of the treatment room before the next client arrives. She has also invested in a large, comfortable and fully electric treatment couch, making it possible for elderly, infirm or injured clients to get on and off the couch with ease.

From her own experiences, Helena offers the following advice for newly qualified therapists setting up in rural areas.

continued...

○ *Find out what benefits are available to you, not only in terms of health and sickness benefits, but also consider potential sources of finance. The purchase of her couch, for instance, resulted from a grant for the couch from the Business Community Chest, an organisation aimed at providing support for businesses in rural areas.*

○ *Develop or find a support network of some kind to provide help and emotional support such as peer supervision group or indeed a personal supervisor. This can be a very lonely profession.*

○ *A good therapist also needs to look at themselves and their motives for doing treatments. If it is purely for the money, then they won't get anywhere; if it is for self-gratification, again they just won't build up a steady client base or have repeat business. But when they start with a genuine desire to help, then things will fall into place.*

○ *Advertising in parish magazines and local papers plus Women's Institutes or local women's support groups is highly effective as are Yellow Pages adverts. Do not neglect the advertising magazines that go to local private schools.*

○ *Put your business cards in every relevant shop including village post offices; what might be considered dangerous in urban areas does not carry quite the same risks in small communities, however make sure you work safely.*

continued...

○ *Always keep a supply of business cards to hand, you will meet potential clients, other therapists or people with whom you could start a network in the most unusual places.*

○ *Know your limitations and make sure you refer on appropriately if the client needs a different kind of treatment to the one you offer. In a small community, word will get around if you are professional and working to a high standard. Helena gets referrals from many of her local GPs because they know her, understand what she is able to offer her clients and have no reservations about her willingness to set appropriate boundaries*

The product(s)

The next step is to outline the products and services you are offering. Try to be as specific as possible in your descriptions, taking into account the needs of those target markets, so that it becomes clear that you are offering something that is going to be very attractive to them. Ensure you include details about how much your services are going to cost, along with explanations of any deals you are going to offer, such as introductory discounts, special offers and so on. With these special deals, outline the circumstances under which you will use them – is there a time limit on how long they will be used for? Will they only be used at certain times or will the special offer run throughout the life of your business?

Note: You may wish to include a copy of your leaflet, which should include your price list. (See chapter 7 for guidance on producing a leaflet.)

FOR REFLECTION

Many therapists appear to be offering more than one product or service. How could you expand the list of products or services you offer without undergoing additional training?

The competition

Your business plan should show that you have paid a lot of attention to your competition. This involves identifying all those who are offering the same or similar products or services within your area and working out how they are operating. In your business plan you should be able to answer these questions about your competition:

○ Who are they?

○ What are they offering?

○ What are their strengths?

○ What are their weaknesses?

○ What needs are they currently meeting for your target market?

○ How are they not meeting the target market's needs?

○ As a result, what opportunities exist for you, which they have missed?

○ Why do you believe people will want to buy from you rather than your competitors?

FOR DISCUSSION

Are any of your competitors potential allies? How could you turn a competitor into a friend or colleague? What are the benefits of doing so?

The SWOT analysis

Revisit the SWOT analysis you produced in chapter 4, and consider what if anything has changed since you produced it. Can you add anything to it when you think about your business now? Having considered the strengths and weaknesses of the competition in more detail, provide more detail in your business plan about what makes your business special and unique, what would threaten your success and how you plan to minimise your weaknesses, build on and promote your strengths, turn threats into opportunities and take every advantage of the opportunities available to you.

Market conditions

Predicting market conditions is sort of like predicting the weather: you know that at certain times of the year you stand a greater chance of wind, snow, rain or sleet. Your experience with and understanding of the market you intend to work with allows you to predict the most likely times you will be busy and when you will experience slow periods. These market conditions will vary with each target market, although you can expect some crossover.

When outlining market conditions, try to answer the following questions:

○ When are clients most likely to want your treatments (time of year)?

○ What times of day are they most likely to want your treatments?

○ Is your target group 'price-sensitive?'

○ What other general issues will affect the success of the business?

○ From your PEST analysis, carried out in chapter 4, list the additional political, economic, social and technical factors that have the potential to affect your market.

DISCUSSION

Consider your list of target markets. What market conditions exist for each of these groups?

DEFINITION

'Market conditions' refers to the general range of circumstances that can affect the way in which your clients buy your services. Your PEST analysis will tell you what factors have the potential to change these market conditions.

'Price-sensitive' means that the price of the treatment or product is the key factor on which your client's decision to purchase is made.

Explain what you intend to do to minimise the effects of poor spending in slow periods and the effects of the PEST factors. Examples might include promoting to different target groups at different times, changing your work practice to take the variations into account, etc. (Changing your work practice might involve going on holiday in the slow periods, when there is no work, or having non-essential staff on temporary contracts that can be released when work is slow).

Financial forecasts

Use the work you carried out in Chapter 4 to highlight the following figures for the first five years of your business. These should link to the objectives you stated for the business.

○ Expected outgoings for the business on a monthly basis for the first year and quarterly thereafter.

○ Expected income for the business on a monthly basis for the first year and quarterly thereafter.

○ Break-even analysis – the amount of income you need to attract in order to cover all expenses.

○ Full cashflow forecasts for this time period with details of the assumptions on which you have based your projections.

Don't forget to include any information that can help those reading your business plan to understand your financial position. This could include explanations for changes in expected income or outgoings, if there are any expected increases or decreases in these forecasts, explain whether this is going to be because of things like market conditions, marketing efforts you have carried out, a new promotion aimed at another target market, increased expenditure related to new purchases or for other reasons.

Premises, plants and fittings

This section involves you stating clearly where you intend to work as well as your long-term intentions

regarding the venue(s) in which you work. Perhaps you intend to start at one or more local centres with the eventual intention of setting up your own clinic. If so, this needs to be stated here and linked to your objectives. For instance, one of your objectives might be to research possible venues for your own clinic once you have met personal targets for the number of clients you are seeing in a week.

Whichever venue(s) you are working from, indicate the level of rent, mortgage, or costs of upkeep you are likely to incur. If you are renting a room in a clinic, for instance, does your rent include a portion of the bills, or will you be expected to contribute to bills on top of your rent?

Your business plan should also outline any other financial commitments linked to the property or venue you are working from. Questions you may need to answer include

○ If you own or intend to own the property, is it available as a leasehold or freehold property?

○ Are you allowed to run a business from it?

○ Are you committed to occupying the place for a specific length of time?

○ Is subletting allowed if you are going to have to cut short your stay?

If you are running the business from your home, it is likely that your household insurance will be affected. As mentioned in chapter 2, it is advisable that you use the treatment room for more than one purpose (thereby ensuring that you do not incur capital gains tax when/if you later come to sell the house).

Plants and fittings refers to the special equipment and furnishings that you will need in order to carry out the work you are doing, this includes all capital items. Indicate costs as precisely as possible and include everything you can think of. For instance:

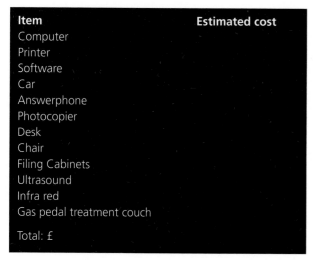

Item	Estimated cost
Computer	
Printer	
Software	
Car	
Answerphone	
Photocopier	
Desk	
Chair	
Filing Cabinets	
Ultrasound	
Infra red	
Gas pedal treatment couch	
Total: £	

How do you intend to pay for these items? Loan/Hire Purchase? Direct purchase? Will you incur interest on it?

Making the business plan work for you

The items outlined in this chapter show you what you would need to have in your business plan. The business plan states your objectives, shows that you understand the market you will be working in, who the competition are and how they work. It also shows that you have worked out how much you are likely to make from the business and when money will be moving in and out of your accounts. Having stated what you intend to do, the next step is to explain how you intend to get it done. This is what is meant by 'tactics.' Your tactics for success should include

○ A detailed marketing plan (see chapter 7 for guidance on producing this)

○ Outline of additional steps you intend to take and when you will do so (for instance, getting a new venue, getting additional training, and so on.

Remember that targeted marketing is the most effective form. As you put together your marketing plan and your tactics for success, remember to check whether the marketing you intend to do is relevant, appropriate and likely to get the best response from the target markets you are aiming at. Keep thinking about what your clients need to hear in order to choose to buy your services and your business will start to work for you.

DEFINITION

'Tactics' means 'actions'. In business terms, it refers to the things you will do in order to get your business to be successful. It can also refer to the contingency plans that you will put into place if you find that the business isn't as successful as you hoped.

Checking your understanding

1. Explain what is meant by a business objective, with examples.

2. What are the advantages and disadvantages to a therapist of being a sole trader?

3. When would it be appropriate for a therapist to be registered as a limited company?

4. What circumstances would make being registered as a charity appropriate to a therapist or group of therapists?

5. Define turnover.

6. What does a PEST Analysis refer to? What PEST factors influence your business?

7. What is a mission statement?

8. What are objectives? What features must they have, if you are going to meet your objectives?

9. What is a target market? What is the difference between targeted marketing and undifferentiated marketing?

10. List the contents of a business plan.

At the end of this chapter, you should be able to

○ Explain what it means to break even

○ Explain what cost-plus and market-led pricing are

○ Work out what price(s) are best for you to charge for your services

○ Explain why you might want to vary your prices

○ Understand how and when to use discounts effectively

○ Predict your sales patterns for the next year

○ Forecast your finances (both income and outgoings) for the next five years

○ Work out your net profit before tax

Introduction

Many therapists report difficulties in managing their finances successfully and with varying reasons for their problems. Some of these reasons are easy to fix; they may have been keeping poor records (or none) so that their accountants have to charge more for the time spent in sorting the problems out. They may not be aware of what they can claim against tax or what benefits they may be eligible for, which could lead to the business being more profitable. They may not be aware of areas in which they could save money, such as buying goods wholesale rather than retail.

Keeping clear and accurate financial records helps us to review the financial decisions we have made, plan for future decisions and analyse what, if any, changes we should make to the business.

Developing your pricing policy

One of the most important decisions you make when you set up your practice is the price that you decide to charge your clients. Many therapists find this a very difficult decision to make as it involves you putting a price on your services and stating out loud how much you think your time is worth. The decision is further complicated by rising costs each year, the very real possibility that you are working in more than one place with different rental or pricing arrangements, and any decisions you might make to have a flexible pricing structure depending on your clients' needs.

One highly successful therapist interviewed argues that you should choose your price carefully and make it a figure that causes your client to wince, but pay it anyway. This particular therapist finds that the success rate of the treatment process is closely linked to the commitment that the client puts towards the treatment and their approach to home care and after-care advice. The price charged, therefore, is an indication of the commitment required of the client to their own health and well-being.

Flexible pricing structures

A lot of therapists choose to allow a certain amount of flexibility into the prices they charge. Reasons for altering your prices might include

- ○ Discounting as a marketing device
- ○ Ongoing discounts for friends and family or those introducing new clients
- ○ Different prices depending on where you work and the costs you incur as a result
- ○ As a policy for special groups – such as the elderly, those seeking work or who are on income support, or where you want additional experience with a specific group (possibly as part of a cancer care support team)
- ○ Where the client needs to have frequent treatments to get the desired result (perhaps you might want to consider offering a discount if they book a series of treatments)
- ○ Where you have had feedback that your prices aren't meeting the expectations of your preferred client groups.

FOR REFLECTION

Can you think of any other reasons why you might vary the price of your treatments?

Cost–plus vs market–led pricing

There are two key methods, or pricing policies, which can help you decide what to charge your client.

'Cost-plus' means that you have worked out how much it actually costs you to carry out a treatment. The 'plus' means that you have then added an amount on top as reasonable profit.

'Market-led' means that you have found out how much all the other therapists in your local area are charging for similar treatments and chosen your price to fit in with theirs. This may mean that you are charging slightly less in order to build up a clientele, or slightly more because you have more experience.

There are pros and cons for both methods of pricing. With 'cost-plus', for instance, you will know that you will cover your expenses with each treatment. This is a particularly useful policy to start with if you are introducing a new form of treatment to clients who have not had access to this before, who have the money to spend and who are willing to do so.

However, if the market place is very competitive, meaning that there are a lot of therapists practising in a similar fashion nearby, you may find that adopting a market-led pricing policy will help you to build up your client list faster. You may find that you don't make quite as healthy a profit on each treatment, but your costs are going to be met over a longer period of time.

Demand-oriented pricing – this means that you have set a price based on what the market will bear – if there is a great demand for your services you can charge a lot, if there isn't, you charge less. You may end up varying your price according to the time of year or even raising your prices as you get more clients. Demand-oriented pricing is most commonly seen with very high profile therapists who may be known for their work on a national or international basis.

For example

Sunita recently qualified as a reiki practitioner. She lives in South East London and has found that the average price for a reiki session in her area is £25 per hour. She intends to practise reiki for one day a week. Before pricing her treatments at the same figure she worked out how much it would cost her to do a treatment. This was done in stages

(a) The kit list – this was a list of all the items Sunita felt she needed in order to practise reiki successfully from home. It included:

Massage table (second hand)	£100.00
Leaflets (to print 2000)	£150.00
Business cards (colour, 250)	£100.00
Blankets for clients	£25.00
Music to play during the session	£30.00
Answerphone to field calls during treatments	£85.00
Uniform	£30.00

The kit list contains items that are going to last a long time; the table will last around ten years, the answerphone will last at least five, as will the blankets and the music. The leaflets and the business cards Sunita is expecting to use up in one year, whilst the uniform would last three years. Sunita then divided her costs down

further so that she could work out how much each item is costing her per month:

Massage table = (£100/10)/12 = £0.84
Leaflets = £150/12 = £12.50
Business cards = £100/12 = £8.34
Blankets = (£25/5)/12 = £0.42
Music = (£30/5)/12 = £0.50
Answerphone = (£85/5)/12 = £1.42
Uniform = (£30/3)/12 = £0.83

(b) Some household expenses that could be charged to her business

A portion of the electricity bill for lighting and to run the washing machine to clean blankets and uniform (£12 per month = £12/30 days x 4 = £1.60 per month)

A portion of the gas bill to heat the room whilst the client was there (£15 per month = £15/30 x 4 = £2.00 per month)

A portion of the telephone bill for dealing with clients (varies according to how busy she is, average of £20 call charges per month of which clients are only 5% of her calls = £20 x 5% = £1 per month

A portion of the mortgage because her business is based in her home* - this to appear as a rent (Sunita decided to charge herself £200 per year as rent = £200/12 = £16.67

*Hint: Discuss this with your accountant or financial adviser. If you choose to charge yourself a rent, you must make sure that the room you work out of has more than one purpose (perhaps it is your living room or spare bedroom), this will ensure that you are not liable for capital gains tax if you choose to move and/or sell your home. Running a business from home also has implications for your household insurance. You must inform your mortgage holder and your insurer if you intend to run a business from home.

(c) Licences and professional insurance: £120.00 per year (£10 per month)

(d) Ongoing costs involved in continuing professional development: £100.00 for two years (£4.17 per month)

(e) Her additional costs of living divided down to a weekly sum, so that she could see how much she needed to earn in order to make ends meet: £200. (If she were working five days a week to earn this, then under ideal conditions she needs to make £200/5 or £40 per day)

(f) Adding all the figures up (except her cost of living) to work out how much her treatments will cost her on a monthly basis:

Table	£0.84
Leaflets	£12.50
Business cards	£8.34
Music	£0.50
Blankets	£0.42
Answerphone	£1.42
Uniform	£0.83
Utilities	£4.60
Rent	£16.67
Licences	£10.00
Ongoing costs	£4.17
Total =	£60.29

(g) If Sunita is practising one day a week, this means that her costs for the day are £60.29/4 = £15.07

(h) Add a percentage on top as reasonable profit and to cover Income tax and National Insurance.

In Sunita's case, matching the price charged by all the other reiki practitioners in her area means that she could add £10 on top of her costs and she has covered her costs for the day on carrying out the first treatment. She also decided to put aside 25% of any fee towards paying her taxes, as this would more than cover her expected taxes. 25% of £25 is £6.25. So for the first treatment – £25– (£15.07+ £6.25) = £3.68 and Sunita only earns £3.68 above her treatment costs. However this small figure doesn't disturb Sunita as she then realised that any subsequent treatments are far more profitable. After the first treatment she will make a profit of £25–£6.25 = £18.75 per treatment

(i) Relate this to her other living costs. Having already worked out that she needs to earn £40 per day just to cover her living expenses. Sunita worked out the number of treatments she needed to do in order to cover her living expenses on top of her costs for treatment: £18.75 x 2 = £37.50; £18.75 x 3 = £56.25. This means that for Sunita to cover all her costs she needed to carry out four treatments a day (cost of carrying out treatments + cost of living).

Why bother doing the sums?

Going through this process helped Sunita to see where she was going and how she was going to get there. It also helped her to make more meaningful objectives as she put together her business plan. In Sunita's case, she came to the following decisions:

○ Whilst she intended eventually to leave her job, she couldn't afford to until she reached a point where she was averaging at least five treatments per day for her reiki days.

○ Although she preferred the idea of working from home as she knew it was more cost effective, Sunita decided she would also look for a nearby clinic or therapy centre to work from as she felt she needed to increase her range of clients faster than she would be able to reach them herself (either via friends and family or through leafleting).

○ She also decided to look more seriously at her personal costs to see if she could reduce them somewhat to make the business more profitable, but without feeling that she was going hungry.

○ She decided to review her marketing more seriously to make sure that what appeared to be a very large cost to her was working well and getting her the return that she wanted.

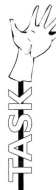

TASK

Develop a kit list of all the items you need to practise effectively. This might include things such as massage tables, uniforms, towels, possibly even a car if you are planning to run a visiting practice. If you are selling products, you will need to include the cost of these in your kit, as well as any additional requirements such as homeopathic remedies, essential oils, infra red or ultrasound equipment and so on. Remember to take into account how long these items are likely to last you.

FOR DISCUSSION

What other items would need to be taken into consideration as you set your price for treatments? Should you include the cost of electricity, heating, your professional insurance or any other items? Is this necessary if you are working from a venue?

FOR REFLECTION

How much will it cost you as a therapist to carry out a treatment? How does this compare with the prices that other therapists are charging in your area? How many treatments would you have to carry out in order to cover all your personal costs?

⬤ DISCUSSION

What advice would you give to a new practitioner if, on carrying out their sums, they discovered that the costs of doing the treatment are higher than the price that other practitioners in the area are charging? What could they do to make sure that they are still able to make a profit from treatments?

Special offers and discounts

Discounts and special offers are used in every business at some stage or other. The temptation to use them regularly can be huge, however, successful businesses tend to be very discriminating about how and when they use discounts; special offers have to be 'special'. Using them too frequently or for too long can adversely affect your profits. Discounting was previously mentioned as a potential marketing method. We use discounts in marketing for the following reasons:

○ as a means of attracting clients who might otherwise not try the service

○ to prove to these clients (and to others) that the product or service you are offering is excellent value for money *at the usual rate*. Ideally the client will want to book another treatment straightaway, even if they don't get the discount they just received.

○ to introduce a new product or service – in celebration of its launch

○ to reduce excess stock (a useful idea if you are selling products and the demand for these products isn't as high as you hoped)

○ to compete with other products or services that threaten your share of the market (see chapter

10 for further ideas about handling threats to your business).

If discounts are going to work for you and not harm your profitability, it is advisable that you use them carefully. You may wish to consider

○ only using introductory offers for a specific time period, say a maximum of three months

○ making sure that, even after the discount, your costs are covered. (If we use Sunita on page 91 as an example, an introductory offer for her should not go below £15, so that she still covers her treatment costs, even if she only does one treatment per day at the discounted rate.)

○ getting your clients to work for the discount – perhaps they need to get someone else to book a treatment with you if they are to receive their discounted treatment, or that the discount is available if they book a series of treatments and pay up front

○ what your purpose is in offering a discount and adjust the terms of the discount accordingly

○ publicising the discount or special offer appropriately – no one will take it up if they don't know about it.

DISCUSSION

How could you adapt a special offer to appeal to the following groups:

(a) New clients that have not tried your services before

(b) Existing clients who would benefit from more frequent treatments

(c) Existing clients whom you haven't seen or heard from for at least five months

---

TASK

Visit a supermarket and identify the range of special offers and discounts used there. Remember that supermarkets are going to have slightly different reasons for offering the discounts they do, but, like you, they still need to make sure that they make a profit, that the customers feel they received value for money and that they get customers to return to their shop rather than to their competitors'.

○ What special offers or discounts did you notice?

○ What were the purposes of these special offers?

○ Which special offers were you most interested in? Did these involve products you have purchased before or ones you had never tried?

○ How could you adapt these special offers to your own practice?

Why did you choose the supermarket you went to? The reasons you give in answer to this question are some of the factors that influence your purchasing decision. Whilst as therapists we may not wish to compare ourselves to supermarkets, our clients will still be making choices (about whether to have a treatment, how often to have it and whether to choose you or someone else) based on their views of the services we offer. Do you feel that you offer those same reasons to your clients (as to why they should visit you rather than other therapists)? Are you making these reasons clear in your promotional efforts? Are there other reasons that would influence the clients you hope to reach?

FOR DISCUSSION

What is meant by 'value for money?' What features would you expect from a treatment, which would make you feel you were getting good value for money?

Predicting sales patterns

Once you have carried out your market research into your clients' needs and desires (chapter 4) and looked at the circumstances that might influence their purchasing decisions, it becomes possible for you to start to predict how and when you will see changes to the numbers of treatments you do; not every therapist is going to be working at full

capacity all the time, and certainly new therapists can expect that it will be a slow process before they will be working at full capacity. Making predictions about how and when you will be working allows you to

○ anticipate busy periods (when you will need to work hard and perhaps limit your social commitments to meet your clients' needs)

- anticipate slow periods (when you might want to book holidays)

- budget to ensure that you are financially secure during the slow periods

- predict how much you will have to save during busy periods in order to cover yourself during slow periods

- identify when you will need to promote your services in order to minimise the effects of slow periods. This might also help you decide what kind of promotion you will need to do.

Every business can expect some fluctuation in their sales patterns. As a new therapist, one of the ways you can discover where you might expect fluctuations is to watch how other therapists in your area are behaving. When do they go on holiday? When have they got special offers available? How easy is it to get an appointment with them? Does this change with time?

Fluctuations in sales patterns will depend heavily on the factors that influence the client's purchasing decision. See chapter 4 for details on identifying these factors in your chosen client group. Because these fluctuations vary widely between client groups, you will often see therapists trying to attract more than one distinct group of clients so that they can minimise these fluctuations and aim for a steadier income as a result.

In order to predict your sales patterns, you need to

- identify the likely busy and slow periods you will be facing

- determine how many treatments you are likely to make during the working day in busy, average and slow periods

- multiply these by your treatment fee to get your likely income for these times.

For example
Oscar has just started work two days a week as a

massage therapist at a local sports centre. Having done his market research, he believes that

- he will experience slow periods for between six and eight weeks during the summer, when his clients are booking their own holidays and during all school holidays

- he will experience busy periods just before school holidays, Christmas and Easter, as the majority of his clients are mothers with children and these are particularly busy and stressful times for them

- his working day will mirror his clients' diaries – although he has access to the treatment room from 8 am to 6 pm, he is unlikely to get appointments booked first thing (prior to dropping children off at school) or after 3.30 pm (following the children's return from school).

Oscar made a couple more assumptions before working out his sales patterns. These included

- a slow day would be two treatments that day, whilst a busy day would be seven treatments

- although the 'busy' day would still not represent full capacity, he felt that 70% was the most he could hope for as a newly qualified therapist working in a busy sports centre

- he anticipated that it would take at least three months from starting at the sports centre before he began to get close to 'busy', regardless of his clients' diaries, simply because he was a new service on offer

- he was not going to take any discounts into consideration on working out his sales patterns as he felt this would be misleading

- he was prepared to do treatments back-to-back and during the traditional lunch hour, at least for the first two years, in order to meet his clients' demands. He would not allow himself a rest when working in the centre, although his work in other venues would be structured differently.

> **Poor week (20% capacity)**
> 4 treatments (2 people x 2 days) @£30 per treatment = £120.00
>
> **Average week (35% capacity)**
> 3 treatments on 1 day, 4 treatments on another = 7 treatments @ £30 per treatment = £210.00
>
> **Good week (50% capacity)**
> 5 treatments x 2 days = 10 treatments @ £30 per treatment = £300.00
>
> **Excellent week (70% capacity)**
> 7 treatments x 2 days = 14 treatments @ £30 per treatment = £420.00

Oscar started at the sports centre in September. Given the figures that he had developed above and his assumptions about busy and slow periods, he decided his first year of sales from that venue would be as shown:

> September – November inclusive = Poor sales x 12 weeks = £120 x 12= £1440
>
> December = 2 good weeks + 2 poor weeks = (£300 x 2) + (£120 x 2) = £840
>
> January = 4 poor weeks (no one would have any spare cash following Christmas) = 4 x £120 = £480
>
> February = 1 poor week, 2 average, 1 good (school holiday approaching) = £120 + (£210 x 2) + £300 = £840
>
> March = 1 poor + 3 average (more people becoming regular clients) = £120 + (3 x £210) = £750
>
> April = 2 good + 2 average (Easter holiday) = (2 x £300) + (2 x £210) = £1020
>
> May = 3 average + 1 good = (£210 x 3) + £300 = £930
>
> June = 2 good + 2 average (school holiday) = £1020
>
> July = 2 good + 2 poor = (£300 x 2) + (£120 x 2) = £840
>
> August = 4 poor (school holidays) = £480
>
> Total: £8640

DISCUSSION

What could Oscar do to improve his bookings? What other client groups could he attract who would a) be willing to receive treatments during the day and b) not be subject to the school holidays?

REFLECTION

Do you think Oscar has made appropriate assumptions prior to working out his sales patterns? Do you think he has been realistic in anticipating how long it would take to get busy?

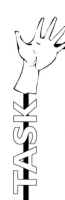

Predict your own sales patterns. What assumptions have you made about busy and slow periods? What factors, including people and circumstances, are you depending on to make sure these sales occur? (The lack of these factors would go into the 'Threat' column of your SWOT analysis, see page 3 for further details.)

Financial forecasting

Financial forecasting takes your sales patterns one step further. These forecasts help you to predict both your income and your expenses over time. This becomes essential information if you consider that some expenses will require payment up front, even if the therapist has chosen to average out the cost of the item(s) over time as they work out the cost of a treatment.

Financial forecasts are a required element of any business plan. Your bank, accountant and financial advisers will want to see that you are thinking about your expenses and income in advance. They will want to see that you are committed to your business, intending to make it grow and that you are able to predict how fast it will grow with reasonable accuracy. Financial forecasts usually involve predicting sales and expenses over a five-year period. They become even more interesting after you have been in business for a while as you will then be able to compare your forecasted figures against what actually happened. This helps you to predict more accurately what will happen to your business in the future as well as giving you a clear idea of when finances will be most difficult, so that you can plan appropriate action.

In order to predict the flow of your finances as accurately as possible, you need to work out the following:

○ Expected outgoings for the business on a monthly basis (you started working this out when you worked out the costs of a treatment. All you need now is to consider all your likely bills and when they are due to arrive, instead of spreading the costs over the entire year)

○ Expected income for the business on a monthly basis (your predicted sales pattern). Look at it again to make sure you feel you are being realistic.

○ Break-even analysis – the amount of income you need to attract in order to cover *all* expenses.

If you are not sure how much income to predict, use your list of objectives (see chapter 5) and your predicted sales patterns and carry out the following exercise:

i)   State desired annual income (for the business) to be achieved within three years of trading.

ii) Divide this number by 12 to get a monthly figure.

Income	Annual Total Forecast	Annual Total Actual	January Forecast	January Actual	February Forecast	February Actual	March Forecast	March Actual	April Forecast	April Actual	May Forecast	May Actual
Aromatherapy	£8,640.00	£8,210.00	£480.00	£300.00	£480.00	£330.00	£720.00	£450.00	£1,050.00	£1,250.00	£900.00	£1,000.00
Homeopathy	£4,620.00	£5,050.00	£360.00	£240.00	£360.00	£240.00	£450.00	£300.00	£420.00	£600.00	£270.00	£480.00
Products	£830.00	£1,600.00	£60.00	£50.00	£80.00	£75.00	£45.00	£100.00	£100.00	£150.00	£50.00	£100.00
Total	£14,090.00	£14,860.00	£900.00	£590.00	£920.00	£645.00	£1,215.00	£850.00	£1,570.00	£2,000.00	£1,220.00	£1,580.00
Expenditure												
Rent	£4,320.00	£4,860.00	£360.00	£360.00	£360.00	£360.00	£360.00	£360.00	£360.00	£420.00	£360.00	£420.00
Utilities	£624.00	£528.00	£52.00	£52.00	£52.00	£52.00	£52.00	£52.00	£52.00	£52.00	£52.00	£52.00
Telephone/Fax	£240.00	£208.00	£20.00	£21.00	£20.00	£21.00	£20.00	£21.00	£20.00	£20.00	£20.00	£20.00
Consumables	£120.00	£559.00	–	£30.00	£30.00	£24.00	–	£35.00	£45.00	£45.00	–	£25.00
Stationery	£152.00	£214.00	£5.00	£7.00	£5.00	£7.00	£10.00	£36.00	£25.00	£20.00	£12.00	£20.00
Marketing	£500.00	£525.00	–	–	–	£45.00	–	£100.00	£25.00	£20.00	–	£20.00
Insurance	£120.00	£140.00	£120.00	£140.00	–	–	–	–	£25.00	–	–	–
	–											
Accountancy Fees	£200.00	£280.00	–									
	–											
Total	£6,276.00	7,314.00	£557.00	£610.00	£467.00	£509.00	£442.00	£604.00	£527.00	£577.00	£444.00	£537.00
Income less Expenditure	£7,814.00	£7,546.00	£343.00	£20.00	£453.00	£136.00	£773.00	£246.00	£1,043.00	£1,423.00	£776.00	£1,043.00
Balance carried forward			–	–	£343.00	£20.00	£1,116.00	£226.00	£2,159.00	£1,649.00	£2,935.00	2,692.00

Figure 6.1 Comparing forecast and actual figures helps you predict future financial patterns. What advice would you give Carmel? Where could she make savings? How or when should she concentrate on attracting more income or clients?

iii) Subtract the monthly outgoings from ii) – this will give you an indication of the profit you are likely to make on a monthly basis, assuming that your outgoings are stable.

iv) Referring to your decisions about how you will be pricing your products, indicate how much you will have to sell, or how many days you will have to work in order to generate the figure set out in ii).

If you are still happy with the figures that you have stated in the exercise above and you think it is a workable option, then the numbers indicated would constitute a **'good'** month for you: business is booming at that time!

Using the figures you came up with when you worked out your pricing policy, repeat part iv) to show:

(a) the minimum you would have to work in order to **break even** in a month – when you just cover your expenses but do not save anything

(b) what you would consider an **average** month – perhaps you are not working to full capacity due to illness or some other unforeseen event

(c) what you would consider a **bad** month – perhaps when expenses are unusually high or when clients aren't paying on time. (Remember that this could be worse than the example for Oscar's income as you need to subtract your expenses from your income.)

FOR DISCUSSION

Sally has just worked out her financial forecasts and is feeling depressed. According to her calculations, she won't break even until she is doing five treatments a day at full price (no discounts), which she believes won't happen until she has been in business for six months as her intention is only to do mobile treatments, visiting people at their homes. You double-check her figures for her and discover that she is charging the same price as therapists working in a nearby health centre. What advice would you give to Sally? Is there anything else she could do to improve the financial picture?

Your taxes

When it comes to finances, your best source of support and advice is your accountant. Choose this person carefully and, if you don't feel you are getting the service you want, find someone else. Every therapist working in Britain must pay tax on their earnings (income tax) and must also contribute towards National Insurance. National Insurance contributions will take the form of paying a Class II stamp. Your Accountant can help you arrange

payment of this with your local tax office. National Insurance payments will involve a small weekly amount being removed from your business account, usually by direct debit.

The amount that you are liable to pay in tax depends on the format that your business takes (sole trader, limited company, etc) as well as how much the business makes. In many countries you will find that there are different tax bands available, so you are taxed at different rates depending on the amount you earn. In Britain, taxation starts at the Basic Rate, which is 25% of your earnings above your threshold of £4000 (this means that you only get taxed on what you earn after the first £4000 after your expenses). Once you, the individual, earn over £40,000 (to check) either on a PAYE basis or again after expenses if you are a sole trader, you are subject to the higher tax bracket of 40%.

Some therapists choose to become registered for value added tax (VAT). This means that your prices must include a portion which is a VAT (in Britain this is currently set at 17.5%). Businesses earning over £37,500 are expected to be VAT registered. Before you earn this figure it is up to you whether you choose to be VAT registered or not. The benefits are that you can claim back all VAT you have spent yourself on things like petrol, capital equipment and so on. The drawback is that you will be spending more on accountancy fees as you will be putting your accounts into the tax office on a quarterly basis to show the VAT you have invoiced for and claimed back.

Bookkeeping hints and tips

Keeping records of your income and expenditure will be something you either love or hate. Either way, it must be done. Your accountant or local Business Training and Enterprise organisations can give you detailed advice on how to make bookkeeping a reasonably stress-free experience. In the short term, you can make the process easier and less costly for yourself in terms of time, energy and accountants' fees if you consider the following:

○ Keep all relevant receipts in envelopes – one envelope per month. Even if it takes you a year to get round to putting the books in order, you will still save yourself time.

○ Write on the back of a receipt what you need the material for (or the category that it relates to). This is very important if you can't work out why it is relevant at the end of the year

○ Keeping and filing your receipts, plus other bookkeeping or administrative details, will take you on average two hours a month. Plan this into your schedule so that you don't avoid doing it.

○ File receipts in date order at the end of each month. Small receipts relating to the same category could be stapled to a sheet of paper marked with the category they relate to and then filed in a larger folder.

○ If you have access to a computer and are computer literate, you could also include a print-out of all the expenses you have had, listed by category, broken down on a monthly basis. This saves the accountant time and you money. Use a spreadsheet program such as Excel to produce this.

○ If you are running a larger business and would like to make the bookkeeping even easier to handle, consider investing in specialised accounting software, such as the Sage package.

○ Discuss the relevant categories you will be filing receipts in with your accountant. You may use all or some of the following categories or other additional categories: Materials, Consumables, Salaries, Rent, Electricity, Heating, Insurances, Postage/Stationery, Equipment repairs, telephone, Travel, Marketing, Miscellaneous, Continuing professional development.

What kinds of things can you claim back on your accounts?

Equipment - couches, cars, answerphone, filing cabinets, cassette player

Expendables - towels, couch roll, oil, tapes, clothing (uniforms and uniform shoes)

Travel - to and from clients, includes petrol, parking, etc

Training - not all, but some, check with your accountant

Professional subscriptions - insurance, training materials (books!)

Publicity - marketing leaflets, business cards

Stationery/Postage - letterhead, paper, files, pens, answerphones, tapes

Overheads - laundry, rent, electricity, telephone

Identifying sources of financial help

Financial help can take several forms, it can either involve finding additional sources of funding or grants available to support your new business. Or it can involve finding training and individuals who can help to make the financial side of your business easier to manage. A selection of potential sources of help includes

○ Job Centre – the Department of Social Services does a good employment training scheme for individuals looking to set up their own businesses. It covers everything you need to know about business finance, administration, marketing, etc.

○ Your accountant

○ Citizens Advice – these can give you useful hints and tips ranging from suggestions for names of accountants in the area, the key council services who can help you identify what legislation is affecting your practice or whom you have to speak to in order to get a licence to practise

○ Training and Enterprise Council – a great source of training and business development courses, advice and guidance. There are similar organisations set up in your local area. Check with Citizens Advice and in your *Yellow Pages* for further details

○ Your governing body – the professional organisation(s) you are affiliated with can give you a certain amount of advice about how to organise your finances as well as offering you guidance on getting professional indemnity, product and public liability insurance

○ Professional magazines – the magazines sent out by or affiliated with your profession will often have articles in them about issues related to business practice. Check the classified advertisements for potential workshops or training sessions

○ Tax Office – The Tax Office has telephone help lines and a range of offices open for public enquiries, where you can go in and get personal help with how to file your tax return

○ The Bank – Each bank has small business advisers, their services are free so use them! Put together your business plan and get them to look it over. They can arrange overdrafts and loans. You also need to open a business account so that you have a registered account, which is what you will be taxed on. Check all the banks for the deals they are offering.

Monitoring your results

No matter how detailed you make your forecasts, you will still find that they don't match what actually happens. Monitoring your financial situation regularly – considering both your income and your outgoings and comparing them with your forecasts – will give you an accurate picture of what is going on. From this you will be able to see

- if you tend to be optimistic or pessimistic in your prediction of sales
- whether you over-estimate or under-estimate your expenses
- when you are likely to have larger expenses than usual, such as an advertisement to pay for, or a tax bill due
- how these figures change over time

Monitoring your finances regularly means checking your expenses and your income on a monthly basis (if not more frequently). Checking them against your predicted results helps you to identify when things are going amiss – if expenses are too high or sales are too low – and gives you the information you need to take appropriate action. Perhaps you will find that sales aren't going as well as predicted despite the promotion you have done. Under these circumstances you might wish to look once more at the nature of the promotion you did and whether it was appropriate for the clients you are targeting.

If the opposite is true, and your sales are far better than you imagined they would be, then monitoring your results will give you the good news very quickly. At this point you may wish to review your marketing as well; what worked for you and why? How can you continue to get it to work for you?

Monitoring your results is an example of good business practice at work. However, this alone is not enough. If you have planned thoroughly and appropriately as you set up your business, you will have an idea as to what you are going to do with the information once you have it. You will also have budgeted for an emergency fund, which you could use to carry out any corrective action required.

DISCUSSION

Think about your own practice and the clients you want to attract. What contingency plans would you put into place if your preferred marketing methods didn't work? How would you know they didn't work? What would you do if you hadn't put aside a sum for emergencies?

REFLECTION

Consider your first year's sales, or if you haven't been in business that long, consider the sales patterns you have so far. Are you becoming more successful at the rate you predicted? Is it slower or faster? What did you do to make this so?

Expert Witness: **Working with International Athletes**

Julie practises and teaches sports massage and remedial massage in West London, as well as working for the Rugby Football Union treating the professional and international referees at Twickenham at each international game. She advises those who want to work with high calibre athletes to "network like crazy".

❝ Newly qualified therapists need to be prepared to badger people for opportunities, to do the work without payment or for very little payment in order to get the hands-on experience needed before they can really start to earn what they are worth. My first job in this field was with an amateur hockey team for which I was paid around £5 per hour. It was eighteen months to two years before I really started to earn a reasonable hourly rate, and I know some therapists who don't manage that for up to five years.

I first started at Twickenham during the Rugby World Series about five years ago, when one of my colleagues who works with the England team asked if I would be interested in joining the medical team providing additional support to those teams who didn't bring a full complement of therapists with them. Unfortunately, on that occasion, there wasn't much work for me to do, so I networked like mad, and in the process got talking to the Referee Development Officer, and, following one of his suggestions, started treating the referees. Things have progressed from there; I suppose it all involved networking, seeing an opportunity and grabbing it. ❞

continued...

In Julie's case the opportunity was the referees – whose changing requirements weren't being addressed. As the rugby teams become better, the referees have needed to become fit enough to keep up with the action on the field. Part of their development as professional referees involves the same kind of rigorous training that the players get in order to keep them on the ball.

" *When I started working with the referees, no-one else was offering this service, although there were sports therapists working with the teams. Now, some of the bigger clubs are providing treatments for the referees, but it is still an unusual practice.*

Treating the referees on match days has now extended to seeing them before games and to a number of them coming to me for regular treatment. It was through one of these regular clients, a touch judge, that I was able to extend my practice into treating the referees through Sevens tournaments as well; hard work but very rewarding. Treatment days at a Sevens tournament means six hours of constant massage with a half hour break at the most. And the referees do take full advantage of the service.

Whilst the atmosphere at a big match is amazing and it's wonderful to feel involved in this way, it is also incredibly difficult to get on to the bottom of the ladder in this kind of business. Most sports teams and sports organisations will be happy to take your services whilst you are training or when it is free, but massage walks the line between a necessity and a luxury; you will be the first to go if there are cash flow problems, and that is mainly because you aren't a physiotherapist. "

continued...

With three children aged 10 and under, Julie stresses the importance of having a supportive partner or network if you are going to work as a body therapist.

> *I thought that sports massage would be something I could fit round the family, and I have been lucky because to a certain extent it does, but it also eats into the time you have with your partner. Most of my clients want treatments in the evenings and at weekends, and I really need to build up a more extensive list of daytime clients now.*

Julie has tried marketing her services in a number of different ways, but maintains that, for her, networking has been the only working solution. Leaflets, she says, were a disaster. She had a large number printed and stuck them everywhere – doctors' surgeries, at the hospital where she was renting a treatment room, in health stores, and so on, but from the first print run of 500 leaflets, she received only two phone calls, one of which was dodgy.

Julie argues that, in whichever way you choose to market your services, you need to be persistent. She felt most comfortable with the networking and it paid off for her.

> *If you feel strongly about leafleting, it can work for you, but you must persist with it, keep leafleting, try new outlets, visit the previous ones with new leaflets, but keep doing it, until eventually it sinks into the client's subconscious.*

continued...

Persistency and consistency are also the qualities Julie feels are necessary in an effective and successful practitioner. Persistency in order to establish your business, and consistency in order to maintain the high levels of service required.

" *Massage is such a personal thing, people take ages to find a massage therapist whose style of working suits them, and if they like you, they stick with you. They also like to know that the person who is dealing with them has a background knowledge and understanding about their personal circumstances. Effective practitioners need to keep their client notes up to date and detailed. When you do, and when you have been working with someone for a while, you will be able to tell instantly when there have been changes to their circumstances – if their skin or muscle tone isn't responding normally for them, if their gait has changed, or much more.*

Consistency also involves continuing to develop your professional skills. I feel that if my students leave the course waving their qualification and thinking that this is enough to practise from for the rest of their working lives, then I have failed as a teacher. People need to leave their initial training courses eager to continue to learn, never to rest on their laurels, there is always room for improvement if you are going to offer a consistently high level of service. "

Checking your understanding

1. What are the benefits of having a flexible pricing structure?

2. Define cost-plus pricing

3. Define market-led pricing

4. What is demand-led pricing? When could you apply this to your work?

5. Compare demand-led pricing and competition-led pricing. When might you want to adopt one of these policies?

6. List the expenses you can charge to your business

7. Under what circumstances might you offer a discount?

8. Refer back to chapter 1 on legislation, what do you need to do to make sure you are not breaking the law when you offer a discount?

9. What figures do you need to look at in order to predict your sales patterns?

10. What is the difference between predicting sales patterns and producing a financial forecast?

11. What does it mean to 'break even'?

12. Why should you monitor your financial results?

7 Managing your public image

Objectives

At the end of this chapter you should be able to

○ Explain what is meant by the marketing mix

○ Explain the additional things you consider when planning your marketing mix, if you are providing a service

○ Explain what a critical success factor is and give examples from your own circumstances

○ Define AIDA

○ Explain what makes an advertisement effective

○ List the various marketing methods available to you

○ Explain which method works best in what circumstances and why

○ Explain the difference between a 'feature' and a 'benefit'

○ Draw up a marketing plan

○ Identify what you need to do to promote your business more effectively

○ Write your own promotional material that reflects your business vision and matches the needs of your target market

Introduction

Marketing is one of the most important activities that you can engage in to make your business work. Once you have worked out your ideas of what you want to do (your business vision) and how you want to do it and what you need to do it (your business plan), you need to get started on your marketing in order to tell your potential clients about your business so that they can start beating a path to your door.

In general, it is wise to put aside between 6% and 10% of your earnings in order to pay for your marketing. This number will change at various times in your career; you are likely to spend more as you start up your business or when you introduce a new product or service; but could spend less as your business becomes more successful. Try not to get complacent with your marketing when you get to a point where the client bookings are looking healthy; marketing still needs to be done to maintain the business, but at this point you might change the methods you use to promote the business.

Many therapists make the mistake of producing one beautifully produced, all-purpose leaflet that remains unchanged throughout their career (apart from altering prices) and doesn't seem to get the results they want. The important thing with marketing is to look at the range of marketing **methods** available to you and the range of marketing **tools** you can use with respect to your product or service and match these up to the clients you intend to promote your services to. For best results, use more than one tool or method to reach your clients.

DEFINITION

A marketing method is an activity you carry out in order to promote your business. For example, producing a leaflet and mailing it out (direct mail), writing an article for the local paper, or placing an advertisement at the corner shop.

DEFINITION

Marketing tools is another term used to describe the marketing mix. The marketing mix includes the four Ps: Product, Price, Promotion and Place. Therapists should add People, the Physical environment and Process to this list.

The marketing mix

Sometimes referred to as marketing tools, the marketing mix is a group of four (or sometimes seven) topics that the therapist can alter to make their product or service more closely meet the needs of their clients. Altering these things can increase the success of the business and can give you the competitive edge you might be seeking to make your business vision come true. Sometimes these changes can spark renewed interest in your business or can give you access to a whole new range of clients. These topics are

○ Product – what you are actually selling

○ Price – how much it costs

○ Promotion – Any special offers as well as the way you describe your product

○ Place – the general location in which the treatment takes place, as well as where any promotional literature is stored or displayed

A business selling a service (such as therapists) should also consider

○ People – everyone involved in interacting with your potential customers

○ Physical environment – the actual treatment room

○ Process – the treatment itself.

Looking at the marketing mix item by item can help us to identify exactly what actions can be taken to promote your business effectively by

○ enhancing your strengths and increasing opportunities for new business

○ reducing the potentially damaging effects of any **factors critical to your success**

○ pinpointing exactly which changes you need to make in order to meet more closely your clients' expectations, needs, wants and desires (chapter 9)

○ saving you time, money and effort, because you might not need to change everything or produce every kind of marketing item in order to meet your clients' requirements.

Critical Success Factor – these are the elements or market conditions that are critical to the success of your business. You can identify these from looking at your SWOT analysis – in particular at the Threats and Weaknesses areas (from chapter 5) and your PEST analysis (chapter 5). The Critical Success Factors are the items on those lists that could either make or break your business. They could include the things or people on whom you are depending most (these may be included amongst your Strengths or Opportunities), so that if they let you down in some way, you won't be able to make the business work.

TASK

There are many ways in which you can potentially alter each aspect of the marketing mix. The following questions suggest a few possibilities. Consider these questions in turn, thinking about the quality of the service you offer your clients now and what you think they would expect to receive if they were to feel that they were getting an excellent treatment that exceeds their expectations. (Hint: You may find it useful to refer back to your SWOT analysis or to the market research you carried out into your clients' needs, wants and desires.)

Product

What is different about the treatment you offer when you compare it to that of your competitors? Is it longer than average? Or shorter? Are the timing and availability of the treatment important to the client? (For instance, do they want treatments during the day or after office hours, and are they prepared to book in advance or do they prefer to appear at the last minute?) Is your ability to stick to the allocated time important to the client? Do you have particular areas of experience or interest, such as sports injuries, skin conditions, digestive difficulties, weight loss or gain, or fertility issues? Can you offer more than one kind of treatment, or can you combine different methods of treatment? What level of care can the client expect from you? Is this different from what they currently ask of you? Is it different from what you would like to offer?

Price

Do you have a range of prices according to the services you offer? Do you/are you prepared to work on a sliding scale, charging different prices according to your client's circumstances? Will you accept payment in kind (and is this clearly stated in your literature)? If so, how much of your work is based on payment in kind? Are your services priced at a level where the client could buy on impulse or are your desired clients more likely to need time carefully to consider the purchase of your services? What does the client get for the price? Is this similar or different from what they might expect elsewhere?

DEFINITION

Impulse purchase – where the client buys your product or service without really thinking about what they are doing or why. With an impulse purchase, price is usually low enough so that the client doesn't hesitate to buy.

Promotion

Does your promotional literature reflect the unique selling points of your business? Does it project the image that you want it to? Do you have any special offers available? If so, what are they? Is your potential clientele aware of these special offers? What forms of promotion and marketing are you using? (Are these reaching the clients you want to attract? (See chapter 4.)

Place

Where will the treatment take place (the venue, not the treatment room specifically)? Does the price reflect this? Is it well maintained? Is it the kind of place where people would expect to find your treatments being offered (so you might get some passing trade)? Is it easy to get to? Is it in an area with which your clients are familiar? How far is the client prepared to travel in order to have this service? Do you have access to some kind of waiting room? What about parking facilities? Bus services? Where are your promotional items in relation to the place? Are they easily obtained? Do you have more than one place where you can display promotional items?

Passing trade/passing traffic – where potential new clients might be passing the place that you work from and stop in to enquire or book treatments.

People

Try to identify all the people that interact with your potential clients and who could be involved in altering their opinion of you and your services for better or for worse. Who are they? Are there any that you don't know of who might be helpful (perhaps specific members of staff at a health food shop, not just the person you spoke to initially)? Are they aware of what you offer? Do they know where you provide your treatments? Are they in favour of your work? Have they tried it themselves? Has it helped them?

Physical environment

The physical environment in which your treatment takes place is potentially one of the easiest items to control about the treatment (assuming you are allowed to make adjustments to the physical environment of the treatment room in the event that you are working as an employee or hiring space). When you consider the physical environment, think about how your client's senses are greeted when they walk into the room and how you want them to view the room:

Sight – what do you see first? Does the treatment room appear clinical, friendly, inviting, home-like? What is the lighting like? What is the colour scheme like – is it restful, vibrant? Does the place look clean and well maintained? Is it private? Can people see into the treatment room? How about the room layout? Does it look cluttered? Is it easy for the client to move around?

Sound – is it noisy or quiet? Do you use music whilst working? Is this music to the liking of your clients?

Smell – does the room smell inviting or noxious? Can you smell things like animals, chemicals, cigarettes, food or other unpleasant fragrances? Is the room aired or stuffy?

Touch – is the room warm enough? What furniture will the client be sitting or lying on? Is it comfortable, clean or easy to manage? What about any fabrics or clothing you supply? Are they clean, soft, comfortable, dry or less than desirable?

Process

Process refers to all aspects that the client experiences in coming to you for the treatment. As well as including the issues listed in the 'Product' section, this will include your consultation process, how you meet and greet the client, the treatment, any additional benefits you offer your clients (such as home-care products or after-care advice), how you complete the treatment and say goodbye to your client, how payment is asked for and received and any follow up that you do. Consider the following questions:

How long does it take you to do a consultation? Can this be shortened in any way if the client is in a hurry? Do you allow extra time on the first visit for a longer consultation period? Do you charge accordingly for this? Are any of the questions on your consultation sheet potentially intrusive to the client? Could they be phrased differently? How do you welcome the client? How do you explain what the treatment will involve prior to their arrival? How do you handle the client – do you need to touch them at all as part of your treatment? If so, then are you gentle or firm in your touch? Are your hands cold or warm? Does the treatment appear hurried or relaxed to the client? What is your body language like? What do you do at the end of the treatment? Do you find your clients need additional benefits at the end of a session (perhaps a glass of water, access to the toilet, time to sit for a few minutes before leaving the premises)?

The marketing mix in practice

It is important for you to meet your clients' expectations in all aspects of your business, from the moment they first hear about you to the point at which they are booking a second or subsequent treatment. Think back to the consumer buying decision (chapter 4) and to the research you did into what your clients want. These two aspects can give you an insight into which elements of the marketing mix are going to be most important to you.

For example

Gloria has chosen to concentrate on treating very elderly clients living within a 30 minute commute of her home. Having done her research into her clients' needs and expectations and considering how they made decisions to purchase a treatment, she made the following decisions:

○ Product – would only be available in the daytime

○ Price – was a sensitive issue, many of her clients didn't have a lot to spare, so she would have to keep her personal costs low so that her services were affordable

○ Place – transport issues were key, many clients needed help getting to where she worked, so she decided to change her practice from working at home to working in a salon in the centre of town and running a mobile practice servicing the care centres, retirement homes and hospices

○ Promotion – her promotion efforts would have to concentrate on the places that she worked from, access issues, the benefits of specific interest to the elderly. It also needed to be clear, simple and easy to read

○ People – as well as thinking about the clients themselves, she needed to concentrate on all those involved with working with or caring for the elderly, including those running the centres she wanted to work at, and charitable organisations supporting the elderly in her area. She decided that she had to think more carefully about how to contact them

○ Physical environment – access was extremely important. She needed to ensure that any treatment room was on the ground floor of the building, or that there was wheelchair access, that comfortable waiting facilities were available and that toilets were also located nearby

○ Process – she needed to allow extra time getting the client ready for treatment and ready to leave at the end of the session

○ Initially, although she had to change how and when she was treating as well as the duration of the treatment, it was most important that her promotion was relevant and interesting for the clients and that prices were clearly stated and visible as these elements were important in getting the clients to make the decision to purchase. She also felt that extra time spent in providing information about her services – possibly with demonstrations at some of the centres – would be necessary to get the clients to book, and made allowances for this as part of her marketing plan.

DISCUSSION

What else could Gloria consider in order to make her treatments particularly appropriate to the clients she wishes to treat?

How would you suggest a new therapist alter the marketing mix to meet the needs of the following potential client groups?

(a) **Commuters**

(b) **Eczema sufferers**

(c) **Keen cyclists**

(d) **New mothers**

Marketing methods

Having looked very carefully at each item in the marketing mix, the next step is to consider the marketing methods available to you, and think about which methods are likely to be most effective at reaching your ideal clients and are still going to be within the budget you have set for your marketing.

Marketing methods to choose from include:

○ word of mouth

○ advertisements

○ articles about your work in trade journals, consumer magazines, newspapers

○ display material (such as posters, business cards or leaflets)

○ exhibitions

○ working through professional organisations

○ networking with other professionals to get referrals

○ relationship marketing

○ direct mail

○ e-commerce/websites

○ sales representation.

DEFINITION

direct mail refers to any item advertising your services that is posted out to somebody. You can do 'blanket' mailing – which means you mail it to everyone possible, perhaps posting it through every door within a 20-mile radius; or 'targeted' mailing – where you send it to specific people whom you can identify as being part of your target market, such as sending it as a leaflet inserted in a magazine aimed at elderly people in your area.

Advantages and disadvantages of different marketing methods

Marketing Method	Advantages	Disadvantages
Word of mouth	The best selling tool of all (if it's good) People listen to people like them Usually gets a faster response (if it is positive) Tends to be remembered for longer Necessary if you are trying to get others to encourage people to buy your services – a key element involved in relationship marketing	You can get bad reviews You can't control it
Advertisements	High profile – generally looks professional if properly done Give impact Create awareness and interest, especially if you use something visual or you word the advert well Simple response required – make sure your details as to how they can find you are included Great if you can sell your service with a simple message	Don't use if you have a complicated message Space usually limited Product could be difficult to express quickly May be advertising in the wrong place Can never tell how effective your advert is
Articles/press and public relations	Works if you have a story to tell that is newsworthy or ground-breaking in some way Raises your profile in the community Necessary if you need to fix a situation where you have experienced bad publicity Easiest to get coverage in local newspapers, but the same rules apply; the information must be newsworthy and of interest to the people who read the newspaper	Profile stories are irrelevant unless you have achieved some level of notoriety within the community at which the article is aimed Won't be covered if what you are doing isn't unusual

Marketing Method	Advantages	Disadvantages
Display material	Can catch the attention of passers-by Generally eye-catching if done well An opportunity to quickly sum up the key points of your business Should be changed often to tap into any seasonal interest or special promotions you are running Must be in good condition and maintained	A waste of time if displayed in the wrong place Where it is displayed will also reflect on your business Sloppy, unprofessional or damaged display material won't sell your services
Exhibitions/local fairs	Generate local awareness/Interest Let you find out what other therapists in your area are doing Work best if the exhibition has a theme relevant to your interests or work Let you meet potential customers Demonstrations could be possible, but are dependent on the venue	Standard of the fair may vary widely Interest or attendance may be low or scattered Costs of attending may be high Venue may be difficult to manage or display your material in, or impossible to handle demonstrations through Theme of event may be irrelevant If carrying out demonstrations, may need another person to handle bookings or enquiries
Through professional organisations	Establishes your professional credentials Possible opportunities to participate in larger, national exhibitions or events Clients will have a proven interest and knowledge of your treatment process, so no need to explain in the same level of detail prior to treatment Possible group discounts on advertising or professional marketing efforts Networking opportunities with your colleagues	Clients will be comparing you with all your competitors in the area Clients likely to assume that what you offer is exactly the same in every way as what your professional colleagues offer. Any competitive advantage could be lost
Networking	Builds up your support mechanisms – vital in circumstances where you are mostly working independently Opportunities for surprising and interesting outlets to work from May help you get to where you want faster Needs you to be very good at explaining what you do, quickly and simply	Requires constant effort on your part May take some time to pay off May need to provide your services free or at a heavily subsidised price for some time in order to get the business you want (this will depend on exactly what your target markets are)
Relationship marketing	Similar to networking, but also includes building relationships with everyone who may be involved in the process of your business, not just the ones who have access to or obvious influence with the people that you want to work with	Time consuming Must be maintained constantly, do not slack off with this Should be of mutual benefit to all concerned. You will find yourself promoting their interests as well

Marketing Method	Advantages	Disadvantages
Direct Mail	Can reach a lot of people easily Can allow for more detailed explanations If targeted, can get to exactly the people you need to Need to research your market and mail at the best times to get them to respond Can follow up on interest or mail more than once When timing is right can be very effective Helps you maintain relationships with existing clients or prospects and keep them informed of changes to your services	Inaccurate or unreliable mailing lists Blanket mailing can be expensive and ineffective Expect a poor response rate (1–2% is about average) May end up mailing at the wrong time Could be that you are sending the wrong kind of detail – perhaps the reader would respond to different types of benefits
E-commerce/websites	Looks professional and up-to-date Allows people outside your usual area to access information about you and your services Opportunities to link your sites to others serving the clients you want Can be as simple or complex as you wish – so you can add more information about your services if you need to Opportunities to sell products through your sites Set up costs can be kept low with access to inexpensive software or where the website development service is part of a package offered by your internet provider You can collect information about clients visiting your site (including their email address) and send them further details as appropriate	Requires a high level of technical expertise (or access to this expertise) to maintain Needs regular updating to appear fresh, interesting and newsworthy and to encourage people to continue to visit the site Links to other sites must be relevant Other sites might not want you to link to theirs Selling products through the website will involve credit card transactions. These must be secure, so additional expense and technical support is necessary Your prospective clients might not be internet-friendly or likely to access the internet in order to find your website
Demonstrations	Allow you to launch new services – any new skills Captive audience with definite interest Allows personal contact with potential clients, so they can see what you are like before agreeing to try a treatment Opportunity to answer any questions in person and allay any fears	Need heavy promoting beforehand to get the audience May need to be repeated at intervals to attract clients from their busy schedules May need to adapt them according to the audience – requires you to think on your feet Needs you to be confident about public speaking, not easy for the nervous
Sales representation/ pyramid selling	Gets other people to sell your products or services for you Increases the personal element of selling, so the sales person is actively promoting your interrests	Can be very time consuming. Look for clauses in any contracts, you may be agreeing to more involvement for less gain than you imagine.

With most of the markets you will be trying to reach, it will be necessary to use more than one method of marketing, possibly adapting your approach to your desired clients according to the situation. Let's look at a few examples of how and when you might use the different techniques.

Advertising

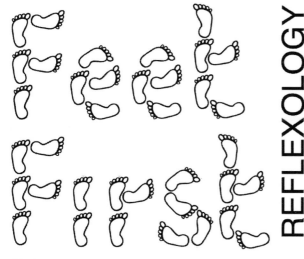

Ring 445287 and ask Frank for more details

Figure 7.1 A sample advertisement

Short, eye-catching advertisements could be placed in your local newspapers, parish magazines, *Yellow Pages*, any community magazines or perhaps in commercial magazines that go specifically to your target market. For instance, if you were interested in attracting the elderly, you might be able to place an advert with a magazine that is delivered to the elderly in your local area. Health and fitness-related magazines also regularly carry advertisements from health practitioners and therapists. Do not allow yourself to be put off by the appearance of the magazine or think that it might be too expensive for you to advertise in it. Most magazines and newspapers offer a range of different prices to prospective advertisers:

○ Lineage adverts – these might appear as part of the classified section. A lineage advert is paid for by the number of words (or lines) that you include in the advert.

○ Display adverts – which involve your advert appearing with a border around it, possibly in a different typeface or with the text at a different size. Display adverts will often include pictures as well and appear alongside an article in the newspaper or magazine. With display adverts, you pay for a set size of advert, often measured either as a fraction of the page, or by single column centimetres.

○ Special features – if the newspaper or magazine is running a special feature on, for instance, complementary health, back pain, fertility, or some other subject that is of interest to their readers, the advertising department will often aim to get new advertisers with a proven interest to place an advert with them, so that readers get information about where the services being referred to in the articles might be available. At these times, the price of an advert can vary – either going higher, if demand for advertising space increases, or lower, if the advertising department has had little interest from advertisers, has too much space to fill and the deadline is approaching. Many newspapers and magazines plan their special features a long time in advance; it is worth your while to investigate potential places for you to advertise and find out how much an advert costs. Even if you initially decide that it is out of your price range, if you know when any special features are going to appear, you can try to budget accordingly.

○ Black/white vs colour – generally it will be slightly cheaper to book an advertisement that is only printed in black and white, not in colour. If you choose to advertise in colour, make sure you pay to have the advert professionally designed, as a poor design can make your advert look untidy and may be a waste of money for you.

○ A run of adverts – advertisers usually get discounts for booking a run of adverts (where they promise to advertise a number of times with the same magazine or newspaper during that year). Discounts can be significant if placed in this fashion.

Remember that the price of advertising in newspapers and magazines will also vary according to the following:

○ print run – how many copies of the magazine are printed and sold

○ subscription base – how many named people have the magazine sent to their homes

○ whether the magazine is bought or sent free – if it is bought, this suggests that people choose to read it

○ who reads the magazine – the advertising department should be able to give you quite a lot of information about what they know of their readers.

As well as advertising in newspapers, journals or magazines, you may be able to place an advert in any local information services, or on bulletin boards at your local library, doctor's surgery, health centres, sports centres or even on noticeboards in office buildings in the local area.

Direct mail

Direct mail is the polite term for 'junk mail' – usually involving unsolicited leaflets. A blanket mailing would be if you had your leaflet inserted in the local paper for your area, so that everyone who received the paper, also got your leaflet. You might use a targeted mailing which would be if you were taking over a massage practice from another therapist and you wrote to inform all her previous clients (who have a proven interest in massage) that you were taking over from her.

Direct mail can sometimes be seen as an alternative to advertising, not only does it allow you to say more than an advert does, but it can sometimes be cheaper to do; for example inserting a leaflet into a magazine before it is published. Most magazines will specify certain conditions about the leaflet if it is to be inserted. These usually relate to the size of the leaflet (generally smaller than A4) and the weight of the leaflet (usually less than 10g – about the weight of one piece of A4 paper). The price of these insertions is usually quoted per 1000 leaflets inserted and there may be a minimum number that you can insert.

Identify three newspapers, magazines or journals that are appropriate to your target market (meaning that the clients you want to attract are likely to read these items). Contact each one and find out

○ **how much it costs to place an advert**

○ **how much it costs to insert a leaflet**

○ **whether they have any special instructions about the size or weight of the leaflet to be inserted and what the minimum number to be inserted is**

○ **whether they can specify how many or which people reading their magazine will get your leaflet.**

Compare the figures you have found – what would you choose to do? Did they offer you any special deals or mention any relevant features coming up that might be of interest to you?

Hints and tips: Most magazines and newspapers will have a website that displays their advertising rates and data. However, you can also visit your local library for further information. Two excellent sources of information in the UK are BRAD – British Rates and Data (which gives readership details as well as advertising rates for all publications) and PIMS – Press Information Management System, which gives contact details for journalists at each source. PIMS is more useful if you are intending to send out press releases or engage in publicity of this nature.

Exhibitions and local fairs

Attending exhibitions and local fairs can be a great way to attract attention and interest in your business. In either case, the way you present yourself and your business is extremely important. The display you put together needs to be eye-catching and generate you enough potential clients to justify the cost of the

exercise. Remember the costs involved in this case could potentially include all of the following:

○ cost of having a space (or stand) at the exhibition/fair

○ cost of any materials you need to purchase to make your stand eye-catching

○ your time in attending and working at the stand

○ lost business because you weren't working elsewhere at the time

○ possibly someone else's time also working at the stand or replacing you when you take a break

○ any advertising you did in the exhibition handbook

○ any leaflets you produce to give away to interested people

○ cost of delivering you and your belongings to and from the exhibition.

To make the exhibition work for you, make sure you know exactly what you hope to get out of attending. Most of what an exhibition is about is to advertise your goods and services to those attending. You can make your business look more interesting and, at the same time potentially generate enough money to cover your costs (even if you don't get many new clients from the event) if you can include some of the following elements:

- ○ products for sale (don't forget to include your contact details on anything sold)
- ○ demonstrations of your skills – short treatments in public, even if you can't take a full consultation at the time, will help clients to understand better exactly what your business is about
- ○ Colourful displays – or something else that will engage their senses
- ○ Making sure that your stand is in an easily accessible part of the exhibition. Good choices are those near (or directly opposite) the entrance/exit, near any seminar rooms (if this is an important element of the exhibition), or near the food/drink outlets (if the exhibition is an all-day event).

If you are interested in attending one of the larger, national exhibitions geared at those with a strong interest in health, beauty or complementary therapies, as an exhibitor, it is worth your time to visit the show first and see what it is like, to make sure that you and your services will fit in and that the people attending the show are the ones that you want to attract to your business. If this is the case, the next step is to enquire from the organisers as to the price of attending. For national shows where there is a strong interest from the public, the prices for having a stand can be significantly higher than in any other situation. You may wish to contact your professional organisation or governing body to see if they are attending and either participate on their stand or find out what they will be doing to promote individual members' services. At national exhibitions, there are usually a number of organisations that specialise in providing an information service, including providing display space for leaflets or business cards at a price. You can get details for these companies from the exhibition organisers.

Expert Witness: Using Public Relations to Support your Business

Sarah Nelson combines her massage practice with working as Public Relations (PR) Manager with one of Britain's largest charities. With over five years experience in 'reputation management' – the definition given to PR by the Institute of Public Relations, Sarah has sound advice to offer for any therapists wanting to use public relations to enhance the success of their business:

" *In practice, PR covers two types of marketing activity; firstly media relations which means targeting newspapers, magazines, radio or tv with stories about your business to get journalists to write about you; providing an unpaid form of advertising which publicises your business, attracting custom and enables you to improve your revenue.*

Secondly, PR can mean those activities that take you and your business into direct contact with the public. This could include having a stand at local exhibitions or trade shows where you think potential customers would be visiting or putting up posters in relevant locations such as cafés, doctor's surgeries or setting up a website.

If carried out effectively, PR can be a relatively cheap way of marketing your business as there are few costs associated with it, unlike advertising or direct mail, which can be expensive to do and difficult to continue to carry out effectively. Building up relationships with local or national press can reap rewards that mean your business will become well known on many levels, particularly to customers or potential business partners.

continued...

If a therapist is really serious about PR and wants to invest some money, employing a PR agency to carry out a campaign with the press on their behalf can be beneficial. A figure often used as a benchmark for agencies is that they should deliver three times the cost of their services in coverage in the media if you were going to spend the same amount on advertising. (This means that the costs of adverts covering the same amount of space would be three times what you are spending on paying the PR agency.)

From a defensive point of view, should anything bad happen to your business, knowing how the media works can help you to minimise any potential damage in the press and ensure your work is not threatened.

If you want to get press coverage, the most important things to do are as follows:

①   *Identify your chosen media, who reads them and the journalists who work for them in order to understand what they want. This helps you to make your story relevant to them and increases the chances of its getting written about. You need to carry out research, buying a few issues of the publications or watching/listening to a few of the tv/radio programmes where you would like to get coverage to make sure they are the right place*

②   *Make sure you identify the right journalist to send the information to within the publication*

continued...

③ *Tailor your material to make sure you take their particular interests into account*

④ *Make sure you really do have a story. Don't expect that just because you think something is interesting or newsworthy, it will necessarily be the case*

⑤ *A lot of PR is about getting rejected and it's important not to see it as 'free advertising' or to expect that it will work in the same way. By becoming a bit thick-skinned about being turned down the first few times, you can learn to give journalists information that is interesting and useful to them, hence getting you coverage*

⑥ *Most journalists are very busy. On average, they probably receive around 200 press releases every day so you need to make sure they will be able to see why the information you send to them is immediately relevant and interesting. Otherwise they will probably ignore it. Many journalists have to write a certain number of articles per day. So if you call with an irrelevant story they will not want to waste time on it – that's why you need to make sure that the story you have is going to appeal to their audience*

⑦ *Timing. If you call a journalist to find out whether they are interested in writing something about you, make sure you choose a good time to do so by finding out when they are on deadline and don't call then.*

continued...

PR is about reaching people with information. The most effective media is the one that reaches the most people who will be interested in the service you offer. For example, the Daily Telegraph *has a circulation of nearly two million, and many radio/tv stations have very high audiences, but not all will be interested in getting complementary therapies treatments, even if the journalist is interested in covering the story, you would get a relatively low ratio of people reading the story being converted into new business. However, a local newspaper or a magazine that is specifically aimed at people interested in complementary therapies or lifestyles, and is probably read cover to cover by people who might buy your service, will get a different response. Don't feel that local or trade media are somehow less important than national newspapers; it's just not the case.*

Generally, you need to be prepared to send journalists a succinct summary of your story in the form of a press release and to be able to talk them through the key points quickly. An effective way of approaching the press is to send information through on email, in the post or by fax. Then find a good time to phone them, asking them whether they've received it, whether they think it's of interest to them. If not, ask what could you do to improve the story?

continued...

A press release needs to be simple, to the point and not include information just for the sake of it – don't use three words where one will do. A simple rule of thumb is that in the first paragraph you should include who, what, when, where and why, and expand on this information in the rest of the press release. A good way to find out what sort of thing to include is to visit the websites of other companies and have a look at their press releases. You should also include your contact details prominently so that the journalist can get in touch with you easily if they're interested in following up the story.

PR is useful when you have something to announce – like a new service or if you want to raise the profile of your business. If you don't have any news, you might be able to approach the media in a number of ways – do you have a well-known client who would be willing to be interviewed about the benefits of the treatment you offer? Or perhaps you could persuade a local newspaper to give you a regular column offering advice about what treatments would be useful for particular ailments.

PR works best when used alongside other marketing methods over a long period of time. This allows you to build relations with journalists, who begin to understand your business, why it's relevant and, as well as sending them information, they may begin to approach you for comments on related stories.

continued...

If you happen to get bad publicity, then don't panic! It's extremely unlikely to happen unless it was deserved and there was a real reason for bad press. Although there is a belief that journalists are out to get people or deliberately misrepresent facts, in 99.9% of cases, that's not true. Most don't have any axe to grind and are pleased you can provide them with information that helps them to do their job. It's not in their interests to write articles that aren't truthful because it damages their reputation. So if they get a report of something bad that has happened, like a client who is annoyed with you for some reason, they would investigate it first to find out whether it has any basis in fact. You can use this opportunity to make sure that you aren't misrepresented. If it does happen, familiarise yourself with the content of the article before you do anything else, and find out whether it's inaccurate (in which case you might be able to seek legal damages). If it is accurate, there isn't a great deal you can do. Although corrections are sometimes made, and inaccuracies addressed, unfortunately these don't equate in scale or importance to the initial articles. **"**

Reviews/word of mouth

Word of mouth is the most effective form of promotion available. Unfortunately it is difficult to control and very difficult to get it to work for you. Word of mouth depends on your clients, friends and family to convince others of the effectiveness of your treatments and offer suggestions as to how you could help them as well. Testimonials of this kind can be the last little piece of encouragement that hesitant clients might need to convince them to give your treatment a try. Although word of mouth is difficult to use actively in promoting your business, there are some ways in which you might want to consider encouraging your clients to participate in the promotion of your business:

○ offer clients a free or discounted treatment when they get someone else to book in

○ ask them for a quote about how the treatment made them feel – which you could then add to your leaflets

○ provide them with a promotional item such as a card or flyer that they can pass on to a friend for an introductory treatment.

FOR DISCUSSION

Can you think of any other ways your clients could be encouraged to spread the word about how good your treatments are?

Relationship marketing

Relationship marketing involves developing the links you have with all the people you deal with in the process of marketing your services in order to get clients. Many of these people are not clients themselves. They can include

○ clients

○ influencers (receptionists, professional therapists' associations, organisations specialising in supporting those with particular lifestyles, interests or disorders)

○ people who might refer clients to you (GPs, other therapists)

○ those involved in recruiting people (bosses, managers of health centres, personnel departments in businesses)

○ suppliers (wherever you purchase your products from)

○ internal markets (colleagues at any centres you work with, your friends or family members).

By improving the relationships you have with these people, you can increase the number of clients you have as well as keeping these people involved and interested in your business. Enhancing your relationships with these people, possibly by offering free sample treatments, demonstrations, or arranging informal discussions about what your work can offer them, will keep you fresh in their minds and may lead to exciting new developments. Relationship marketing might use a leaflet, newspaper article or business card as a support mechanism – perhaps to start or end a conversation, or raise a topic, but for the most part this depends on face-to-face, telephone or email contact. Contact is also regular and of mutual benefit.

DISCUSSION

How could you improve your relationships with each of the groups listed above?

Social marketing

Social marketing is seen as slightly different from relationship marketing as it involves ways of marketing your services that are also designed to raise awareness of the treatment process and to make your treatment more acceptable to your target market. This can be a very important task if the treatment process you offer is new to your area, where the potential clients don't understand how it works or where your work might be seen to border on breaking local social or moral customs. Think about how body treatments could be viewed where a community does not allow individuals to be undressed in front of strangers, particularly if they are of the opposite sex. Under these circumstances, you would need to explain not only the treatment process and its benefits, but you would also be faced with convincing your potential clients of your own ethical and professional behaviour. Social marketing, therefore, might involve running small talks, workshops or demonstrations to explain your work and it will involve gaining the confidence and custom of key people whose interest and patronage can positively affect your business.

DISCUSSION

Teleselling involves using the telephone to promote your products or services. You may have already experienced this if your suppliers ring you up to inform you of any special deals they have going on at a particular time. When might you use teleselling to increase interest in your business? Do you think this is an appropriate marketing method for your work?

Practical promotion – hints and tips

Whichever marketing methods you choose to use, you will at some point need to write something about your business in order to sell your products or services effectively. In these cases, it is important to think about the purpose you have in writing. Marketing professionals refer to a process that they want the reader to go through on seeing a poster, advert, or leaflet:

A   Attention

I   Interest

D   Desire

A   Action

Attention

The promotional item should attract the client's notice. You might use eye-catching images; bold, witty or appropriate headlines or colourful paper on which the item is printed. A combination of all three works best. Images should relate to what you are trying to say, should be clear and memorable.

Interest

Whatever you write should be immediately relevant and appropriate to the client you are trying to attract. You hold their interest through making the connection between their personal circumstances and what you have to say. Perhaps you have identified a problem they face, which they weren't completely aware of until reading your material. Now you can go on to present the solution

Desire

The next step is to make your product or service sound so attractive to the client that they have to do something about getting it. You caught their interest by identifying a problem they have. This is the point that you offer the solution (your services) and outline the benefits that you can offer them. If you have done your research into your customer's needs, wants and desires correctly, then the benefits you offer them at this stage will be all they need to pick up the phone and book a treatment.

Action

If the job is done right, you will have the clients beating a path to your door. You caught their attention, identified a problem and offered a working solution. The next step is up to them – to book a treatment. Remember that you need to give them the information required in order to help them do exactly that – and sooner rather than later. It sounds obvious, but make sure that your contact details are clearly written on the promotional item.

Effective promotion is always geared towards the client's needs. When you start to write your material – whether it is a press release, advert, leaflet, or poster, you can expand on some of the questions Sarah mentioned in her press release (above) and aim to answer the following questions:

○ Who	will benefit from the treatment (who are you aiming at)?
	are you (and do you have experience)?
○ What	are you selling?
	can it do for me (benefits to the client)?
○ Where	are you practising/is it easy to find?
○ When	is it available?
○ Why	should I buy it/try it/switch to it (more benefits in greater detail)?
○ How	do I book a treatment?
○ How much	does it cost?

DEFINITION

A feature is an item – for instance a CD player might have a remote control, a skirt has a button, zip and a slit in the back. A massage might feature vegetable oil, Swedish massage techniques, large fluffy warm towels . . .

DEFINITION

A benefit is what it does for you – the remote control means you don't have to get up to turn the CD player on. The button and zip are for decoration, a good fit and/or easy access, the slit in the back is so you can walk/run easily.

The following guidelines to writing can help you to write simple, effective leaflets, adverts or posters

1. Include a headline – this is the one thing you want them to remember, attention grabbing, creates interest, gets them to read on, this is the hook that tells them that something you are offering them is going to make a difference to their lives. For instance, it might relate to the conditions that you are interested in working with (perhaps cellulite or keeping resolutions – both are popular post-holiday topics). Your headline should be large, clear and interesting.

2. Include a couple of second level messages – these are the next most important things to remember. These could be key questions people have about your services (like 'What can Reflexology do for me? or How does it work?) or it could include a list of the key benefits of your work or any special offers you are running.

3. For leaflets only – include full explanations if space allows. This is the material they will read only if they are really interested or uncertain about making an appointment. Make sure that you tailor the material to suit their interests and any worries they might have.

4. Offer solutions, not problems, throughout your work – even though you might have identified a problem that your target audience is dealing with remember that, whilst the insight into their problems might be new to you, they have been living with these problems for some time. They want results – tell them what you can do and explain how and why it will work.

5. Keep things simple – short sentences are easier to understand (you will know far more about your subject than they do), short or commonly used words rather than jargon are also easier to read (your clients might hate going to anyone remotely connected to health – especially doctors – if they are worried that they won't understand what is being talked about).

(6) Be careful how you describe yourself and your treatments so that there is no danger of clients believing you provide any other services apart from the treatment available.

(7) Logos can be used to create an image for your business and to improve people's awareness of what you do. Try not to get caught up in spending a lot of time trying to find something you like. If you do choose to develop a logo, make sure that you can use it easily, perhaps transferring it to your computer so that you can print it out whenever you write a letter.

(8) Miracles can be achieved with fancy paper and a photocopier. If you are unlikely to use leaflets extensively, you do not have to spend a lot of money producing them. Leaflets that have been designed on your home computer and are printed out only when you need them, allow you to change them according to the seasons or the clients you are working with. This also allows you to be more flexible – you may be working from several different clinics for instance. Business cards are also available for production on home computers and can be bought as a sheet for printing out on demand.

(9) If you do not have access to a home computer, you can still use the computer facilities available at local internet cafes or the library. Remember to keep your work on disk so that you can make changes whenever you like.

TASK

Select a range of leaflets or magazine adverts that you like or think are effective. What makes them so? Do they follow any of the suggestions here? What additional information do you think the adverts would need to include if they were going to be turned into a poster or a leaflet? Do you think the leaflet would be as effective as the adverts you like?

Design a leaflet that provides details of your products or services.
Your leaflet should be aimed at one of the following target markets:
Hospitalised, but recuperating, patients

Commuters

Jet lag sufferers

Frequent travellers

School teachers

Those dropping children off at school/PTA members

Neighbours

Local business persons

Small businesses

Holistic/complementary therapists

If you have more than one target market in mind for your business,
then they will almost certainly need different answers to the
questions relating to the benefits you can offer them. Make sure
that your leaflet reflects your unique selling points. Can you now
add anything to your list of unique selling points?

FOR DISCUSSION

Think about the target markets you wish to work with when you start
practising. They will have distinct needs, but also very different interests
and requirements. Which marketing methods would work best for you?
Why?

Drawing up a marketing plan

A marketing plan is literally a list of things you intend to do to promote your work properly to the clients you wish to target. It should reflect the objectives you have outlined in your business plan. If your business plan states what you want to do and why, your marketing plan tells you how you are going to make people aware of your work and how much it is going to cost you to do so. A detailed marketing plan looks a bit like a calendar of events and will include the following:

○ date when marketing action will take place

○ type of marketing action taking place

○ cost of marketing action (both what you have budgeted for and what it eventually really costs)

○ any contingency funds – the amount of money you have put aside just in case things cost more than you anticipate

○ reasons why you are carrying out particular marketing exercises

○ any special messages you intend to promote at particular times.

Marketing plans need regular reviewing so that you know whether you are getting the desired results. As you start your business or introduce a new product, you may find it useful to consider drawing up a marketing plan for the first eighteen months or two years of your business. Refer back to your business objectives. If you have set targets that relate to how much turnover or how many clients you hope to be treating within a given time, then that time limit is an appropriate one to cover with the marketing plan. This will then help you to see whether your marketing efforts are effective at helping you to reach your targets. Monitoring the marketing plan against your business objectives will also help you to see whether your objectives are as manageable and realistic as you initially thought.

TASK

Draw up your own marketing plan. Make sure you include details of all the activities you are planning to carry out and when you intend to do them. Don't forget to budget appropriately for your work. If you are planning to produce a leaflet, for instance, you will need to find out about printing and/or design costs from a local printers, or how much it is going to cost to photocopy your leaflet onto special paper nearby.

Once you have found out how much things are going to cost, it would be safe to add on about 10% of the total costs as a contingency fund. This will allow for inflation or for possible extra opportunities that you haven't planned for but seem too good to pass up.

Hints: Don't forget to use the marketing plan – it won't help your business if it sits in a drawer for six months.

Checking your understanding

1. What is meant by AIDA?

2. What is the marketing mix?

3. What are the extra three things that a service company should include in the marketing mix?

4. What are the differences between a feature and a benefit?

5. What are critical success factors? Give examples from your business.

6. List the advantages and disadvantages of using direct mail.

7. When might you use public relations?

8. What should go into a press release?

9. What is relationship marketing? Who would you have to work with if you were doing this for your business?

10. What is social marketing?

11. Which marketing methods are most likely to be successful at promoting your business. Why?

12. Name the magazines and newspapers that your potential clients are most likely to read. Which ones are appropriate for you to promote through? If none are, explain why not.

Objectives

At the end of this chapter you should be able to

- ○ Discuss the advantages and disadvantages to different methods of working
- ○ Explain which method(s) is best for you and why
- ○ Discuss the importance of good time management and ways of using time effectively
- ○ Handle telephone and personal enquiries effectively
- ○ Discuss how you would handle criticism or complaints professionally
- ○ Explain the importance of being appropriately insured for your treatments
- ○ Outline the different types of insurance and what you would have to do in the event of a claim
- ○ Discuss ways you can ensure your personal safety when working
- ○ Discuss the ways in which you can plan for disaster and the things to keep in place should problems arise

Introduction

You are at the heart of your business, no matter what form it takes and no matter what kinds of client you are working with, the whole experience must work for you and keep you happy and motivated. This chapter deals with some of the logistics you may face as part of your working week and gives you some hints and tips on how to handle them effectively.

Motivating yourself

Every therapist, no matter how experienced, has days when it is really hard to keep going and stay enthusiastic. We all need a great deal of support around us at times like this. However, there are some steps you can take to make it easier on yourself, which will encourage you to keep going:

- ○ Set goals (and objectives) that are meaningful and realistic – don't make the targets too high, you can always adjust them upwards later.

- ○ Celebrate when you get to your goals, even if you are in the process of setting new ones, it is important to recognise your own progress.

- ○ Try to be consistent – in your work and in doing your administration. Even if you hate the admin, doing a bit of it regularly will keep it from running out of hand and swamping you. Furthermore, try to make sure that the last treatment you give each day is just as good as the first one.

- ○ Find ways of boosting your morale – take time out for yourself regularly in order to do things that make you feel good.

- ○ Focus on the positive things that are happening – this is particularly useful if you do this at the end of a hard day, reminding yourself of the good things that have happened will help to put things into perspective.

- ○ Develop your network of supporters, whether they are family, friends or colleagues, whom you can turn to for practical or emotional support.

○ If a problem arises, remember your goals and try to think laterally; there is always a choice of ways around or out of any problem; thinking creatively about a problem or asking advice from your support network will help you to see things differently.

Different methods of working

The way(s) in which you work can be a pleasure, or a disaster, for you if you choose the wrong one or end up with a group of people (or a pile of administration) that leaves you dissatisfied. Each working method has its advantages and disadvantages, a selection of which are listed below.

Method	Advantages	Disadvantages
Working from home	Inexpensive Low overheads Relaxed atmosphere Family/flatmate as receptionist Allows you to manage work commitments around family commitments Flexible working patterns are easier to manage	Family noise Animals have access to treatment room Looks amateur Can be difficult to maintain confidentiality Potential for accusations of assault Possible obscene or inappropriate phone calls to home telephone number Invasion of privacy Increased risk of theft Potentially increased risk to personal security Can be lonely
Salaried in a clinic	Can get either full- or part-time work PAYE – guaranteed monthly income Clinic does all publicity and admin You get paid even if you have no clients Can get additional (free) training Sometimes commissions/bonuses No financial investment required Maternity leave (not always just statutory)	Not as much potential for rewards or for self-development May dislike management decisions or other therapists Contract will often state that you are not allowed to poach clients and work within a certain radius of the business if you choose to leave

Method	Advantages	Disadvantages
Rent a room in a clinic	Low overheads Only take the time you need Can build up clientele and number of hours worked slowly Potential referrals to/from other therapists Not isolated Clinical/professional atmosphere Looks credible Good/bad reputation by association with the clinic and the other therapists there Goodwill of established therapists Receptionist as a buffer for your patients Reception can handle fees if you have difficulty managing this Often some flexibility included in terms of services offered as part of the contract Could work from more than one clinic, therefore increasing range of potential clients	No control over increases to rent charged Limited involvement in managing or organising or decorating treatment room Potential arguments with other therapists or support staff Problems could arise with reception services Obligated to fulfil any contractual obligations, may take some time to get out of the situation if you are unhappy with it
Lease/buy new premises for a new salon/clinic	Can bring in other practitioners Opportunity to share costs Colleagues could act as receptionists Joint marketing reduces costs Sharing or delegating of administration tasks is possible Publicity talks or exercises can be part of a joint effort More control over the working environment You are the boss	Expensive start up costs Rent can be very high, depending on the area you are working with Vulnerable to the landlord's decisions about rent, safety features, plus the nature of the work being practised there. Relies on other practitioners to participate in all aspects of the business May be tied into a long lease May need a substantial refit and refurbishment to turn them into treatment rooms if the premises are not purpose-built

Method	Advantages	Disadvantages
Locum work (covering for therapists on maternity leave or similar)/buy an existing business with a list clients from a therapist in the area	Instant patients Can expand your existing business and that of the person from whom you are taking over You inherit the goodwill the clients offer to your predecessor as well as their reputation in the area Adds credibility to your work by association with the other therapist Short term financial gain (if the business is thriving) Good networking opportunities	Requires confidence and experience to step into another therapist's position Will lose some patients regardless Existing practice and clients' expectations might not be in line with your intentions for the business Initial marketing costs when taking over another business are generally more expensive. Can be for a limited period only, especially if the other therapist intends to return Contract often includes a request that you will not practise in the area for a set period afterwards (for locum work) and that you will not take clients with you when you go
Mobile practice	Keeps your home private Can work with less mobile people Can provide a value added service to the client – they don't need to go anywhere after treatment Can charge more for treatment (to cover timing and parking costs plus use of car)	Needs a car for transport Heavy equipment could cause back problems Security is risky – you need to take added precautions Need to allow more time between treatments for you to get to your next client Less control over the working environment
Hotels	Meeting a large variety of clients Often very good tips Hotel does all advertising and marketing	Limited regular contact with clients Sometimes therapist services can be viewed as a cover for prostitution – so potential misunderstandings from clients The treatment becomes the focus of the client's attention, so limited opportunities for viewing treatment holistically or to suggest home care advice
Airlines	Excellent travel opportunities Can be based on flights or on the ground (in airport terminals) so the amount of travelling you do will vary	Physical effects of frequent flight – disrupted sleeping patterns, potential increased risk of DVTs, and so on Occasionally limited working area No opportunities to develop regular clientele

Method	Advantages	Disadvantages
Spas	Thoroughly professional environment Usually high levels of staff training and top quality equipment Emphasis is on rest, relaxation and well-being Clients are either committed to their own health or experimenting with improving it – so confirmed interest in therapeutic work	Emphasis may be on getting as many clients treated as possible, so little rest in between for the therapist Usually a strong bias to sell supporting products, which some therapists can find difficult to do
Holiday resorts (ski resorts, beach resorts, cruise liners, etc)	Travel opportunities are exceptional Relaxing environment for clients Staff benefits and accommodation can vary widely Can be easy to save money whilst working in this way Equipment, resources and working conditions can also vary	Limited long-term contact with clients, so you can't check the results of your treatment Minimal contact with your home environment, so you can't build up a personal business alongside
With professional sports teams or similar	High commitment levels required May involve extensive travel with the team Will give you a great deal of excellent experience working with performance issues and muscular aches/pains very quickly Will improve your timekeeping and assessment skills Improved access to sporting events Works best if you already have experience, a strong interest in or understanding of the particular needs of the sports professionals you are targeting	A problem if conflicting priorities arise Commitment to the team may mean that other commitments have to suffer Therapist's reliability and commitment may be questioned if they are working with more than one team or group at once Difficult to break into

Which working method(s) are best for you?

① For your business to fit in to your life, use the chart below to identify when you would be able and willing to treat someone. Try doing this first with your existing commitments in place. Then do it again with how you would like to see your work developing (if this is different) (Note: Don't forget to include time off for yourself):

② Consider the criteria involved in working and what is most important to you as well as those methods that will be easiest to set up. Issues to consider include

(a) Environment – is it important to you and your clients?

(b) Pay – do you want a regular monthly income or are you prepared to risk this?

(c) Working hours – do you want a regular slot for clients or are you prepared to work changing shifts? Do you need these to fit around family commitments?

(d) Responsibility – do you look forward to running your own business, do you want to share the management or would you prefer that someone else was in charge?

(e) Contact – how much contact do you want to have with colleagues or other therapists?

Time	Mon	Tues	Wed	Thurs	Fri	Sat	Sun
AM							
PM							
EVE							

Managing your time effectively

Effective time management is like dieting – it only works if you are committed to doing it, convinced it is necessary and if you see results for your efforts.

Most of us waste a lot of time each day doing things we can't account for and then wonder why we haven't finished all the things we set out to do. As a therapist, your time-keeping needs to be excellent and, especially if you are running your own business, so does your time management – if you are going to get things done AND have time to rest at the end of the day.

TASK

How and where do you waste time?

Step 1: On an unconscious level you probably already know what you spend too much time over. The list could include phone calls, supermarket shopping, running errands, etc. Write a list of your main activities (including sleep, washing and dressing) and how much time you THINK you spend on each one during a week.

Step 2: After you write your list, keep a log of what you have done and how much time it took. Start your log from the time you wake up in the morning to the time you go to sleep at night and break it down into intervals as small as 15 minutes. Keep a log like the one below for one week, then compare your results with what you wrote in Step 1. What did you learn? How and where could you cut back on wasted time?

Time	Mon	Tues	Wed	Thurs	Fri	Sat	Sun
AM							
6 am							
6.15 am							
6.30 am							
6.45 am							
etc							

Getting more time-effective

Only you will be able to identify the most appropriate steps to take to free up more time in your personal life in order to make more room for the business. However, here are some proven hints that can help both in a business and a personal context:

- Keep a diary with all your appointments in it, both personal and professional.

- Keep only one diary as you will start to lose appointments or information if you have it in more than one place.

- In a salon, spa or similar environment, it is the usual practice to keep appointments in pencil in case clients need to change their time or day of appointment.

- Work out the time of day you are most and least effective at giving treatments or handling mentally challenging tasks, adjust your schedule to fit your personal preferences. You could use the time you are least effective to do things that don't require much thought – confirming bookings, filing receipts, paying bills or similar.

- Try to handle urgent administration details in short bursts. Non-urgent stuff could be postponed and handled once a week if appropriate.

- Set specific times when you will return phone calls, emails or make calls. The rest of your day is for your other appointments.

- Operate a 'clean desk policy' – even if you don't have a desk in your treatment room, the principle is the same; keep your work area tidy and make it immaculate at the end of the day.

- Delegate where you can – is there someone who might do your shopping for you? Can you arrange delivery of groceries? Could someone relieve you of other responsibilities in the home? Can you order your treatment supplies by phone or over the internet?

- Only pick up a piece of paper once – deal with things straightaway, whether it means replying to or throwing away the correspondence.

- Write lists of things that you need to do, and prioritise them, setting yourself deadlines when you can.

- Stick to time – leave plenty of time to get to appointments on time, and stick to the appointed time for clients; even if they are late, don't run the treatment over into the next session (this will encourage them to be on time in future).

- Be specific about when you are free to do a treatment, allocate your time carefully.

- Block out times to do your treatment, even if you choose not to work back-to-back, arranging to do several treatments close together will help you to develop more efficient working habits.

A strong commitment to time-keeping and time management can benefit you in unexpected ways, some of which include:

- feelings of achievement as you become aware of getting more done in the day

- being better able to stick to the time allocated for a treatment

- appearing better organised and more professional to the client

- once your time-keeping improves, you become more able to do treatments back-to-back if required (or desired) which can in turn make your treatments more cost-effective, especially if you are hiring a room or the venue where you are working

- if options for treatment times are limited and clients become aware of other people seeking those appointments, there is more of an incentive to book repeat sessions early or immediately, hence a more regular clientele develops

- if clients are aware that other clients are arriving within a short time of their treatment finishing, they are more likely to honour your commitments to your other clients (as well as to themselves) by arriving and leaving on time.

FOR DISCUSSION

What other benefits can you think of for managing your time at work effectively?

Dealing with an enquiry

Enquiries for treatments come from all different sources – from people passing where you work, through word of mouth and response to your advertising or promotional material. Dealing effectively with the enquiry involves three major components:

- giving the client the information they need
- establishing whether the enquiry is genuine – and if you are going to be safe and happy to work with that client
- doing both of these things in a polite and friendly manner.

Not every client is going to need a lot of detail prior to booking. Those who have experienced the kind of treatment you offer before are more likely to be interested only in

- the price of the treatment
- when treatments are available
- occasionally in your qualifications and experience
- how to find you/get there (if they don't already know).

Clients with less experience of the treatment may also wish to know the following

- benefits of the treatment specifically to their situation
- what the treatment will involve
- how long it will last and how long the effects of the treatment will last.

FOR DISCUSSION

What other information do you think clients will want to ask you before booking a treatment?

When you take an initial booking with a client, either on the phone or in person, it is very useful to ask a few questions yourself. Not only will these help you to gauge whether or not the enquiry is genuine, but will also give you an insight into your client's expectations:

○ Where did they hear about you? – this will let you know if an enquiry has come through someone you know (word of mouth) or via another form of marketing.

○ What do they expect from the treatment? – this can usually give you an idea of any possible contraindications in advance as well as telling you if the client knows much about the treatment and how it works. It will also let you know if they have less than appropriate ideas about the kind of treatment you are offering.

○ Full contact details – most salons will take just a name and telephone number; this can be acceptable if you are treating in the salon environment and there will be other people around when you are carrying out the treatment. For all other treatments, get the full address as well and, if carrying out a mobile treatment, check it is a real address too.

○ Parking, location and access details – this is only relevant if you are doing a mobile visit and will help to establish how easy it will be to transport you and your equipment to the place you will be treating from.

Dealing with telephone enquiries politely can occasionally be more awkward than dealing with people in person as your clients will form an immediate impression of you from the phone and may pick up misleading information. You can help to make your business sound more professional when you do the following:

○ answer the phone cheerfully, giving your name and/or the business name as you say hello

○ ensure there is no adverse background noise when you answer the phone

○ if working from home, consider either using a different telephone number for your business (which could be set off against your taxes) or arranging with the phone company that a different tone will ring when a business call comes through for you

○ do not pick up the phone whilst you are in the middle of a conversation with someone else or are distracted by events going on around you, this will be obvious to the client and the sense that they are interrupting you could put nervous clients off making a booking

○ use an answerphone when you are with clients or otherwise distracted. You can return calls later

○ if you are returning calls, try to do so within one day of the message being left

○ at the end of the telephone call sum up the key points that the call involved. For instance if you were taking a booking confirm the time, date, venue and price, then check if they need any other information.

Handling criticism

Even the best therapists receive criticism or complaints at some stage in their career. Handling that criticism effectively involves seeking a win-win solution: one that is satisfactory to all concerned – to the client complaining, to the therapist and to the employer (if relevant).

○ Discuss the problem out of the hearing of other clients (if relevant) – the reception desk is not an appropriate place for any problems to be discussed

○ Listen carefully to what the client has to say, feed back in such a way that you check with the client that you understand exactly what they are complaining about

○ If you need to get more information about the complaint, take the client's details, explain what you are doing and tell them when you will contact them to discuss it further. Make sure you contact them as agreed

○ Do not get pulled into arguing with the client. This will not solve the problem

○ Negotiate – find a solution you can both agree on or which follows the clinic's guidelines if you are working in a clinic and such guidelines exist

○ Remember that the appropriateness of the solution is going to vary with the complaint – you may want to consider offering the client their money back, a free or discounted treatment, a replacement treatment with a different therapist, products or gift vouchers, advice or nothing!

TASK

Role play

Each of the following examples are situations where a client might complain. Working in pairs, take turns being the client and the therapist. How would you respond to each of these situations?

Case 1

A client rings two hours prior to a booked treatment and complains that they have incurred 'undue stress' in the process of booking a treatment with you as, because you are so popular and fully booked, they have been unable to get a booking for three weeks, although other therapists are, and have, been available. They want you to give them the treatment free of charge and tell you that, if you won't, they intend to complain to the clinic manager.

Case 2

A client rings you and indicates that they had negative side effects following treatment and now doubt whether the treatment is effective.

Case 3

A client comes to see you and, during the process of the treatment (after it has started), indicates that they have been to see a colleague of yours who practises a different discipline and were dissatisfied with the treatment.

Case 4

A client receives treatment from you and, at the end of the treatment, despite any checks you carried out during the session, indicates that they are dissatisfied with the service you have offered and do not intend to pay for it.

Insurance for therapists

There are four types of insurance that are potentially relevant to you as a therapist. The most important ones, which each therapist needs to have, are professional indemnity insurance and public liability insurance, both of which are necessary in the unlikely event that a client decided to sue you. Employer's liability is only relevant if you have people working for you, and product liability is only important if you are selling products on to members of the public.

Professional indemnity

This insurance protects you should a client decide to sue you claiming they have experienced personal injury or damage as a result of the treatment you carried out.

Public liability

This insurance covers you if a member of the public (such as a client, passer-by or similar) is injured on your premises or if their personal property is damaged in any way.

Employer's liability

If you hire others to work for you, then you need to make sure that your business insurance covers you for employer's liability – so that you are covered should a member of staff have an accident on the premises and attempts to prove that the accident came about as a result of your negligence. The certificate of employer's liability must be displayed in the premises and all such certificates filed safely for at least 40 years.

Product liability

This insurance is extremely important if you are planning to use, manufacture or sell products as part of your business. It will protect you in the event that a client is dissatisfied with the product or experiences a reaction to it, or if the product is in any way faulty.

Personal safety

Your personal safety is a matter of vital importance and should not be taken lightly as you begin to work as a complementary therapist. No matter how professional you are in terms of your appearance, demeanour or your intentions for treatment, there are individuals who can, and may, misread you or your work. Taking sensible precautions can reduce the risk of any danger to you or to those who work with you. The key aspects to maintaining your personal safety involve

○ ensuring that you have appropriate back-up in case trouble arises

○ knowing what you would do if trouble did occur

○ making sure that any enquiry for your services is genuine and that both you and the prospective client know what to expect from the treatment process.

Each of these aspects will vary with the circumstances in which you work. For instance, in a salon or health centre there may be a buzzer or panic button that could summon help if required. At home you might have a neighbour or friend who could act as a receptionist and could either go for help or intervene if you ran into trouble with a client. The most vulnerable group of therapists, those who run a mobile service and make house visits, could either take a companion with them when they do these visits or ensure that they let someone know when they arrive at their destination and when they leave it. In all of the above cases, setting up the treatment space so that you are between the client and your exit could give you the moments you need to escape if this proves necessary.

Think about the way in which you intend to work. What can you do to enhance your personal safety?

A genuine enquiry?

○ Take the enquirer's telephone number and phone them back to confirm the treatment. Contact details will be necessary anyway, not only as part of the consultation form but in case you needed to get hold of them if something happened to prevent treatment taking place. They should be willing to give you the number; if they don't want to give you contact details, treating them may not be advisable.

○ Find out where they heard about your services from.

○ Explain how you work and send a copy of your leaflet in advance of the treatment. Listen to how they respond or question you about your services, making sure that there is no room for misunderstanding. Remember that they may have certain expectations about your work based on the venue that you are working from.

What expectations would you have of a therapist working from each of the following venues? What additional steps do you think the therapist could take to avoid their services being misunderstood?

○ **Home**

○ **A hotel**

○ **A doctor's surgery**

○ **A health food shop**

○ **Mobile practice**

Planning for disaster

Thinking about potential disasters doesn't mean that you will force them to happen. This is like having insurance – if you think about what could possibly go wrong and what you need to do to deal with it, then you can have the structures in place to cope with disaster quickly and successfully.

Some potential disasters could include:

- ○ a client intending to sue
- ○ an accident in the clinic or whilst you are treating someone
- ○ you have an accident or fall ill and can't work for a while
- ○ bad publicity or media coverage
- ○ your personal safety is threatened in some way
- ○ theft of your equipment (or worse, of your client notes)
- ○ another therapist poaching your business
- ○ legislation coming into effect that would mean that you can no longer practise.

FOR DISCUSSION

What other potential disasters can you think of?

Dealing with potential disasters means you need to assess how much you are at risk of the disasters happening. If necessary you may wish to take steps to reduce that risk. Some possible solutions include:

- ○ having a contingency fund – some extra money put aside to cover additional marketing or insurance costs or similar

- ○ increasing your insurance cover – most therapists are insured for around £1million as part of their professional indemnity insurance. You can increase this coverage if you wish

- ○ including health insurance in your insurance cover. Many health insurance policies will cover loss of earnings following injury or severe illness. Having adequate health insurance cover is strongly advised, especially if you are the sole earner in your household, if the business depends on your being fit and healthy and if you are involved in extreme sports of any kind

- ○ developing good relations with the press or media, especially if you are well known in the area. If they have a good relationship with you and they hear about client(s) who are dissatisfied with your work, they are more likely to speak to you first before printing or publicising a story. You may then have a chance to reply or sort out the problem with the client before it becomes public

- ○ ensuring your personal safety by being more observant of your surroundings and looking very carefully at the ways you risk yourself in the course of your work. Take every step you can to keep yourself safe

- ○ insuring your equipment, because theft of your equipment could potentially stop you working whilst you take time to replace it. Make sure all your equipment is covered on either your household or business insurance policy, that it is covered on a 'new for old' basis and that the insurers are quickly informed following the theft and give permission for you to replace your equipment immediately

○ having other therapists poach your business is a sign of unprofessional behaviour on their part and has been dealt with in chapter 3. However, use this action as an indication of some aspect of your business or treatment needing room for improvement. If and when poaching happens, take it as an opportunity to look again at how you work and what you can do to make it better. Remember that, as your clients have come to you for treatments before and given you their contact details, you can approach them directly, perhaps sending a post card or questionnaire about your services (to identify any areas for improvement) or phoning them to see how they are doing and if they wish to book another treatment (as you currently have a 'special offer', perhaps?). This will give them the chance to let you know if there is something they were unhappy with in your treatment. Clients who have decided to go elsewhere permanently have little incentive not to tell the truth about their reasons for going, so you are likely to get a very honest answer. Don't take any criticism of this nature personally, it is offered for you to improve your services with

○ keeping abreast of political changes and what they could mean for you. Get involved in continuing your professional development so that your work is always above reproach.

FOR DISCUSSION

What other methods could you use to reduce the risk of disaster in your working life?

Expert Witness: **Getting Funding for your New Business**

Lucy Aldous is Managing Director of PART, the Portsmouth Area Regeneration Trust, a community development financial institution aimed at helping people either to become self-employed or to start 'micro-enterprises' – small businesses that employ fewer than five people.

" *The term 'micro-enterprises' was developed to get away from the word 'business' and all the scary things that this can mean to people when they first get the idea of going out on their own.*

A lot of companies like PART exist around the country, although you will usually only see them in disadvantaged areas, as they are geared towards helping people who can't access the usual services, either because they have a bad credit history or where circumstances have taken them to the edge, for instance if they are a single mother trying to support a family without help from a former partner or where they have been made redundant through no fault of their own.

continued...

If you need funding to get your business started, then, no matter who you turn to for financial support, you will need to have a business plan and cash flow forecast to show them what you intend to do. The paperwork you produce should include details about your market, where the customers come from, what the demand is for your product or service, who the competition is, what your prices are, what people are prepared to pay and why. It is absolutely essential that you show that you have done some market research, no matter what kind it is – if you are standing on street corners, filling out questionnaires with clients, interviewing people working in other, related businesses, or just collecting leaflets to show that you have found out who your competitors are, what their prices are and what their usps are. Doing the market research will help you to be absolutely clear about what products you are prepared to offer and what you will be doing that is different from everyone else.

Your paperwork must also include details about how you are going to promote your services to your market, what it will look like, how you will get customers and how you will keep them. Don't forget to include information about when you and your services are available and where, and link it in to why your customers will want this kind of service.

The cash flow forecast needs to show not only how much money you need to keep the business going and for you to survive on, but you also need to make sure you have predicted the income you will generate over 12 months, showing any peaks or troughs you anticipate.

continued...

A lot of people get worried about what kinds of numbers they need to show for the figures, but when I am looking at someone's cash flow forecast, what I want to see is that they have worked out how many customers they need per week, how many they are likely to see, how much they will charge for those customers and to show whether they can fit all of those customers in during the time allocated for their business and still make the income they need to survive.

Looking at the financial side of things should also include identifying what your expenses are. If you are worried about how to put together a cash flow forecast, your bank is a great place to start for advice. As well as having small business advisers, they can also provide you with a blank cash flow forecast that takes you through each step of producing your own forecast in advance of asking for financial support.

Once you have gone through the process of producing a business plan, remember that this is not just something that you do for the lender, it should be a document you produce that is designed to help you set your goals and monitor those goals against what actually happens. You may want to think about setting times when you will evaluate what is happening. For instance, if your sales are down, you may need to buy less stock or promote more heavily, or both.

As you start to think about financing your business, shop around for the best deal for yourself. Take your business plans and forecasts to the lender(s) you would like financial support from and leave it with them for a while to look at it in advance of your meeting with them.

continued...

When you go to the meeting, make sure that you present a professional image. That doesn't necessarily mean that you have to wear a suit, but what should come across is that you are confident, know what you want, that you are clear about how you are going to get there and that you are fully committed to the business and to making it happen. If you aren't particularly sure of yourself, at least be sure of your response – so if you don't know the answer to a question you are asked, say that you'll go away and look into the issue raised and respond to it later. If I am considering lending money to a therapist opening a new business, what I am hoping to hear when I ask them what they will do if the business doesn't succeed is a response along the lines of 'this isn't going to fail, because ...'

As well as being very clear about your motivations and your commitment to your business, it is a very good idea to stress the links between your existing experiences and what you intend to do. Even if you are changing everything in your life – maybe leaving the big marketing career to work as a reiki practitioner – mention your transferable skills and how they fit in to your plans for your business.

If you haven't got lots of business experience, it doesn't necessarily mean you won't get the support you want. They'll be able to get a pretty good idea of how you are likely to run your business by talking to you about how you manage your personal finances, so if you develop a personal budget, pay your bills by standing order, check your receipts against your bank statement and so on, they know you are likely to be financially responsible.

continued...

Even if you aren't that good at regularly checking your bank statements, you can still impress a lender with your ability to run a business successfully if you concentrate on the planning and forecasting elements and you emphasise the support you have for your work, whether that support means that your brother-in-law is an accountant or your Mum is going to be your receptionist or that you are getting help from the local training and enterprise units or the Business Links.

Assuming the meeting is successful and you get your loan or overdraft, the next steps are to make sure you pay back the funds on the date that they are due. If you run into trouble with the repayment schedule, remember to keep in touch with the lender – even if you can't pay. As long as communication remains open and they know what is going on, they are likely to be more flexible and helpful. Remember that by lending you money, they have become a partner in your business and they are just as keen as you are to see you succeed in your work.

continued...

The thing that a lot of therapists and other small business owners forget is that this can be a very lonely experience for them. Whilst you are setting up and even after the event, make sure you build up your network of other people whom you can talk to and bounce ideas off. Either use your family and friends if they have appropriate experiences and if they know how to listen or, alternatively, you could check with your local business support services and keep in touch with them about issues that arise. Whilst you will want to keep any employees involved in the decisions you make that affect them, there will be some incidents where you need to talk and there is no one immediately around you to share the discussion with – times when, for instance, you are having problems with a member of staff or even when finances get tight and you don't know how you will pay everyone at the end of the month. **"**

Checking your understanding

1. What methods of working do you intend to practise? What are the advantages and disadvantages of these methods?

2. What specific safety precautions should you take when working in these ways?

3. Which methods of working are least appropriate to your circumstances? Why?

4. How can you improve your time management at work?

5. What information should you get from a client when first taking a booking?

6. How can you ensure that you handle telephone enquiries effectively?

7. What policies exist in your workplace for handling complaints? If you are working for yourself, what policies do you plan to set up?

8. What are the different types of insurance a therapist should have?

9. What additional kinds of insurance might be advisable and in what conditions?

10. What should you do to plan for disasters?

At the end of this chapter you should be able to

○ Explain what is meant by professionalism

○ Explain why hygiene methods are important and give examples of how you can maintain hygiene within your working environment

○ Explain the nature of confidentiality and how you can work to maintain it

○ Explain, with examples, what professional ethics means

○ Discuss the importance of the consultation process and how it can be managed effectively

○ Explain how and when it is necessary to refer clients to a GP or medical practitioner

○ Briefly describe a range of complementary therapies that you might want to refer a client on to

○ Discuss why you need to be aware of contraindications to treatment

Introduction

From the moment your new client picks up your promotional literature they will have certain expectations of you, your behaviour, how their questions and personal details will be handled and the treatment process. A successful treatment to them will be one in which all these expectations are met and during which they experience some benefit from the treatment itself. Meeting all those expectations requires a great deal of attention to detail on the part of the therapist and a thoroughly professional approach, which covers every aspect from personal hygiene and appearance to dealing with telephone enquiries and referring on to other practitioners. Aspects to consider include

○ working in a professional and ethical way

○ respecting the client's personal modesty

○ personal hygiene and appearance

○ hygienic working habits and a hygienic working environment

○ knowing when to refer on to a GP or another practitioner

○ knowing how to listen effectively both during the consultation process and thereafter

○ dealing appropriately with complaints or praise.

Professionalism

As a professional therapist you are expected to give your clients the best possible treatment that you can deliver and to act in a professional manner. Aside from your actual treatment itself, your professional behaviour is also under scrutiny. This means you must:

○ concentrate on the client – leave your own issues outside the treatment room and focus completely on what you are doing

○ think only of the situation in front of you, not the person who is waiting or the one who just left

○ think about the image you want to give people of yourself and the type of practice you run. Check you aren't mixing your messages and that what you are offering suggests a safe, comforting and relaxing environment to the clients you want to attract

○ keep clean. If you work with body treatments it is essential that you wash your hands thoroughly before and after treatment – ideally in such a way that the client knows you have done so. The treatment room must also be kept as hygienic as possible. Suggestions for doing this are listed on page 177

○ develop excellent time-keeping skills. Both you and your client may have other appointments and it is important to honour those other commitments

○ do not gossip at all

○ guard against emotional involvement. This is important. Try not to get involved with your clients on a personal level. It makes it awkward for therapist and client, you run the risk of being accused of harassment or misconduct if they get very uncomfortable. If you feel uncomfortable or you think things are getting out of hand, the best thing to do is refer them on to another practitioner

○ know when to refer on. It is okay to admit that you don't know everything or that the service you are providing may not be the best thing for that client, or that they may need something different. You look professional when you refer on because you are thinking about the client's well-being before your monetary gain

○ build a list of contacts in other therapies in your area. Not only can you refer on to someone you know and trust, but they will often reciprocate – remember that the most successful form of marketing is word of mouth

○ keep clear records of the treatment you are carrying out and any information related to it, including, if relevant, your thoughts and feelings regarding the treatment process. Aim for accuracy and diplomacy here. Remember that your client is allowed to have access to their notes if they ask for it (so don't be rude about them!)

Different client groups may have very different expectations of the treatment space you work in. Which client groups do you suspect would prefer:

○ **A very clinical atmosphere**

○ **A home-like atmosphere**

○ **A spa-like atmosphere**

○ **An atmosphere that reflects alternative spiritual practices**

○ **An atmosphere that reflects the outdoors or an outdoor retreat?**

What things could you do to change the atmosphere of your current (or planned) treatment space to recreate these different atmospheres – and therefore meet the client's expectations? How could you vary things to meet more than one set of client expectations?

Professional ethics

Professionalism also involves being ethical in your approach to your clients, your colleagues and your own career. Every therapeutic discipline is governed by a code of ethics, which can be obtained via your professional organisation or governing body and will usually appear as part of the membership pack. For the most part, you can expect this code of ethics to include the following.

○ Be discreet and respectful – do not discuss your colleagues, other professionals or other establishments.

○ Maintain client confidentiality – do not discuss your clients or their treatment process with anyone else, especially not other clients. Occasionally you may need to discuss the treatment process with other therapists if you need advice on how to proceed, but this should be understood to be of a confidential nature and you must be sure the other therapist is able to maintain confidentiality in turn.

○ Keep all records safe – do not let anyone have access to (or the chance to see) client records apart from the client and you. You may wish to consider storing client records under lock and key, keeping client names and contact details separate from their notes (with a code to identify each client) or similar. If you are keeping client data stored on a computer remember firstly to register under the Data Protection Act and secondly to ensure that your files are properly protected from unauthorised access with appropriate software and passwords.

○ Do not go beyond the limits of your training – treat only in the manner in which you have been trained.

- Do not diagnose – this is the remit of medical practitioners alone.

- Do not claim to cure any condition or disorder, this is inappropriate and contentious.

- If you are referring on to another practitioner, make sure you know how they work and that you like what they do – your opinion will matter to your client. If you can't recommend an individual therapist, pass the client details of the governing body of the discipline you are recommending in order to help them find a therapist, or suggest they contact their GP, who might also be able to recommend someone.

- Your treatments should go alongside any medical treatments and are not to be used instead of them. If your client has specific concerns about advice or guidance the doctor has given them, encourage them to return to the doctor to have their fears allayed, do not suggest or carry out anything that could interfere with the treatment they are receiving elsewhere.

- Keep up-to-date in your chosen profession – most disciplines require that you undergo some form of continuing professional development on a regular basis.

- Display any qualifications as appropriate – this is reassuring to the client and confirms your professional standing and your commitment to the treatment process.

- If the client is concurrently receiving treatment from another complementary therapist, ensure that the therapist in question is aware that they have sought treatment from you. Some therapies don't sit easily alongside each other.

- Make sure you are appropriately insured for the treatments you offer.

- Follow the advice and guidance of your professional organisation, particularly when changes to the way you are expected to work are being discussed.

- Keep up-to-date with current events relating to you and your work (for instance changes to the legislation governing the practice and use of complementary therapies).

DISCUSSION

Which therapies work best alongside the treatment(s) you offer? Which ones don't? Why? What precautions would you suggest that a client be aware of if they were seeking treatment from a discipline that doesn't work particularly well alongside that which they are receiving from you?

DEFINITION

Aseptic – a clinically clean environment – free of infection.

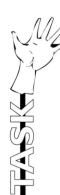

> *Obtain a therapist's code of conduct and professional ethics from your governing body. What other elements are you required to comply with above and beyond the list provided here?*

Maintaining a professional appearance

Your client will have expectations of your appearance and, whilst these can vary depending on whether you are working from home or in a salon environment, it is in your interests to work towards appearing professional during the treatment process. A professional appearance can help you to set and maintain your personal boundaries. A uniform (and it doesn't have to be completely white!) can also be reassuring to friends or acquaintances coming for treatment as they will view you differently, coming to understand that what is discussed with you during the treatment process will stay with you. This will allow them to be more confiding than they might otherwise have been. On a practical note, uniforms are usually hard-wearing and are less likely to be ruined than normal clothing if you are working with a range of products.

A professional appearance can involve the following:

○ Uniform – which is immaculately clean, ironed, easy to take care of, comfortable for the therapist to work in and non-suggestive. If you are working with products, pick a uniform that is 100 per cent cotton as this will respond better to boil washing.

○ Shoes – comfortable, practical with good ankle and heel support and a decent tread, so that you can work appropriately in them and will not slip if the floor is polished. If your treatments will have you standing most of the day, it is a good idea to consider getting an arch support in your shoe as well.

○ Hair – clean, tidy, off the face and, in hot weather, off the neck as well. If you have long hair, wearing it on top of your head is most appropriate so that you are not irritated by it or tempted to touch it whilst working.

○ Jewellery – avoid all jewellery, with the exception of any wedding band. Most jewellery on your hands and wrists will interfere with your work. Fob watches are a useful addition to your uniform if you don't have access to a clock in your workroom.

○ Nails – keep these short, clean, free of varnish and any debris. Remember that if you are applying pressure during body treatments the nails can sometimes be felt by the client and are highly irritating as such. Long nails on a therapist do not inspire confidence in the client that the treatment will be therapeutically beneficial.

○ Clean shaven – male therapists are advised to be clean shaven where possible or to keep facial hair neatly trimmed and cared for.

Personal hygiene in the therapist is also a very important aspect of the professional appearance. If your personal hygiene isn't maintained, it can suggest that the hygiene of the treatment room might not be thorough either. Personal hygiene is going to be particularly important if you are doing body treatments, as you are exerting yourself physically during the treatment and are also coming into close contact with the client. Pay particular attention to the following aspects:

○ your uniform is clean and freshly washed each time you wear it

○ bathe or shower at least once a day, preferably before starting treatments

○ use antiperspirants and/or deodorants on a daily basis

○ if you are prone to sweating, carry deodorant wipes, soap or similar with you and take the opportunity to freshen up before treating

○ if it is hot, or you sweat a lot, keep a face towel near your treatment area in order to pat yourself dry if you are in danger of sweating onto the client. This is a key hygiene issue! Ensure that your sweat or body fluids don't come in contact with the client during the treatment process

○ if you need to blow your nose, cough or similar during the treatment, wash your hands before touching the client again

○ brush your teeth regularly (at least once a day) and use breath fresheners if you suspect bad breath or have eaten strong-tasting foods such as garlic, chilli or curry.

Handling your client appropriately

Client care and client modesty are two aspects of the treatment process that can be essential to meeting the client's expectations as to how you deal with them on a personal level. As you will see from the list of features below, there is a certain amount of overlap between these two issues and the concept of professionalism in general.

Client care refers to the practical steps you take to care for the client's health and well-being before, during and after the treatment as well as the interest you show in their response to the treatment process.

○ Be polite and honest

○ Be organised when they arrive for treatment, so that they aren't kept waiting too long

○ Monitor your time-keeping so that you don't make the client (or yourself) late for their next appointment

○ Treat them with consideration for their physical and emotional health and well-being at all times

○ Ensure that they are comfortable as treatment starts and finishes, paying particular attention to aspects such as heating and lighting in the room, ventilation, noise, and so on

○ Avoid interruptions to the treatment process

○ Develop a relaxing and comforting working environment

○ Maintain hygiene, both on a personal level and within the working environment

○ Watch health and safety issues – so that clients are not going to trip or hurt themselves on anything stored in the treatment room or as you are carrying out the treatment

○ Make sure there are safe, secure and appropriate places for the client to store their belongings whilst treatment is taking place.

○ Keep accurate records

○ Update your qualifications regularly

○ Do not gossip

○ Actively listen to the client and respond to their needs or wishes

○ Check that the treatment is progressing as they expect (in body treatments look for indications of pain or discomfort, for instance)

○ Do not diagnose

- Refer on to other practitioners when you are out of your depth
- Work only with the techniques you know and are trained for
- Help clients onto and off equipment as appropriate
- If appropriate check for progress and reactions to treatment between treatments (or at the next treatment).

Client modesty refers to the steps you take to maintain the client's privacy before, during and after the treatment. This is particularly important if you are carrying out body treatments:

- Do not leave the client physically exposed at any time during the session
- Only expose the section of the body you are working on at the time
- If you need to halt the treatment part way through, remember to cover the client before moving off to deal with the situation as required
- Ensure you have adequate changing facilities for them to dress and undress in private

- If you do not have adequate changing facilities, then develop certain habits to make up for this – for instance appropriate towel management techniques using large bath sheets by preference to give the clients adequate changing space or leave the room whilst they undress. This will be particularly important as they climb onto and off the treatment couch
- Remember to safeguard all client notes
- Consider carefully how you phrase the questions that you need to ask as part of your consultation process, so that your questions are not seen as invasive or unnecessary
- Conduct your consultation process in private where your client's responses to questions cannot be overheard
- Do not comment or pass judgement on anything your client says as part of the consultation process. It may be an issue that is sensitive to them and they need to know they can trust you to empathise with them, not to be dismissive, shocked or horrified.

DEFINITION

Client care – the practical steps you take to care for the client's health, and well-being and their response to the treatment process.

DEFINITION

Client modesty – the steps you take to maintain the client's physical and personal privacy before, during and after the treatment.

Listening to and hearing the client

One of the key reasons many clients seek complementary therapies is that they feel they receive more time, empathy and attention from a therapist than they do if they go to the doctor. Whilst this is not the case with every doctor nor with every therapist, it is true that the average appointment with a GP lasts between five and ten minutes whilst an appointment with a therapist usually lasts at least half an hour.

If we are to build on this, to help make clients feel that they are properly heard and to meet or exceed their expectations for treatment, it is useful to know how to listen effectively to the client and to give appropriate indications that we have heard what they have said and, where appropriate, are prepared to act upon it. Learning to observe all aspects of the client's communication process will also make it easier for you to assess the client at the start of the treatment and to monitor progress thereafter. This takes practice. However, the benefits are likely to spill over into your personal life as well, so you can expect improved communication all round.

About communication

Communication is a two-way process – it is about giving and receiving information, thoughts, ideas and feelings. It involves sending and receiving messages. We need information from our clients in order to choose the most effective ways of treating them, or to find out whether it is safe to treat at all. This means we have to develop ways of being very good at picking up the messages clients give us, and even working out when they might be holding some information back. For example, a client might come to you for treatment for muscular aches and pains in their neck and shoulder region but feel reluctant (initially, until they get to know you better) to tell you about other symptoms or stressors that are bothering them. This reluctance could involve:

○ the belief that you won't be able to help

○ the belief that it is irrelevant to the treatment they are asking for

○ the belief that you are untrustworthy

○ the belief that you won't be supportive or empathic or sympathetic

○ the belief that you are not listening to them or wouldn't be able to understand what they are going through.

FOR REFLECTION

What other reasons could the client have for not giving you the full story?

Communication isn't just about the words we use, most of the message – how your client feels about what they are telling you – is conveyed through non-verbal means. The most revealing non-verbal messages come through

○ facial expression – think about the signs you recognise that indicate if people are happy, nervous, upset, excited, depressed or angry

○ tone of voice – the tone of voice can be used very effectively to let people know you believe what you are saying, that you are happy or unhappy with a situation, to express sarcasm or joy and much more. Remember to check for hesitations in their speech as well. This can sometimes indicate that they are on the verge of confiding in you.

○ body position – the way someone sits or stands, how far away they like to be from someone else, or if they prefer to stand uncomfortably close to others. This also involves how they place their limbs; do they cross their arms over their body, cross their legs tightly, or appear relaxed and fluid in their movements?

○ touch – people have different preferences as to how often they want to be touched or to touch others. This also varies with their emotional state. Be particularly careful about issues to do with touch in the therapeutic situation. In general, therapists tend to touch others more than most people and to assume that this touch is okay with the client (and most of the time it is). Your client has not actually given you permission to touch them until the treatment is taking place, so a smile or a gesture might be just as welcoming, but not as threatening or as open to being misunderstood.

○ body posture – the client's posture can also give an indication of how comfortable they feel and about their emotional state; are they slumped in the chair or sitting rigidly erect? Are they holding themselves awkwardly – which could also indicate physical problems?

○ gestures – take a look at how the client is using their hands as this can also indicate underlying emotional issues. Are the hands folded in the lap, gripped tightly, being wrung or constantly being wiped against the sides of the legs? Are they using their hands to cover parts of their face or nose (this can sometimes indicate lying or uncertainty as to what they are saying or an unwillingness to say it).

Active listening

Outside of non-verbal messages, we need to listen very carefully to what our clients are saying and even to train ourselves to remember the words and phrases they are using to keep our records detailed and up-to-date. This is especially important if your client needs your emotional support and wants you to hear what they are saying; sometimes looking down at your case notes and writing whilst they are talking can be seen as being distracted. Checking their body language and tone of voice will often give you a good idea of when it is okay to continue to write and when you should focus directly on them and stop taking notes for the moment.

As a therapist, you will need to know some of your client's personal details in order to provide an effective treatment. Taking case notes at the beginning of a treatment (the first treatment) and asking how they are feeling (at the beginning of any additional treatments) helps to break the ice and establish you as a professional who is trustworthy. When you take notes about what they have said, you are reinforcing the image that they have of you as someone who listens and is concerned about their needs.

Complementary therapies are most often used as a means of relaxation and stress relief. With physical relaxation, you often get mental relaxation. This can mean that the client will feel less inhibited and may choose to confide in you about issues that might be bothering them. In order to help them effectively, you need to be able to hear what they are saying, understand what they are saying and show that you have listened and understood.

Active listening means that you

○ allow the person to finish what they want to say, without interruption

○ focus on them – make eye contact

○ stop what you are doing to listen to them (although you may want to continue the treatment if they are talking during the session – let them guide you in this)

- ○ encourage them to continue (nodding, encouraging noises)

- ○ keep to the subject, don't divert onto other topics unless they choose to

- ○ don't bring in personal feelings and experiences – whilst it is okay to do this in a personal situation, in a client/therapist situation, remember to leave your feelings and opinions at the door. Concentrate on your client instead.

There are a number of techniques you can use to show that you have been listening and have actually heard what the client has said:

- ○ Paraphrasing – having listened to what the client has to say, respond by starting your sentence with 'So what you are saying is...' This tells the client that you have heard and understood. It also allows you to check that you have understood. The fact that you are attempting to listen to them helps them to feel more positive about what they are doing. Summarising the situation can help to bring clarity to their thinking about it.

- ○ Asking questions that have a purpose – questions that have a substance to them, that aren't aimless. Make sure that these relate to what they are talking about. These can be particularly useful in the consultation process (see below).

- ○ Asking open-ended questions – questions that encourage more than a yes or no answer. These can be used to focus the client's thoughts or to help them feel less threatened by subjects that are difficult for them to talk about. Examples are:

  - ○ focus questions – 'What would you like to happen with (this situation)?' 'What's the worst thing that could happen?' 'If you had to ask yourself one question now, what would it be?'

  - ○ less threatening, thought-provoking questions 'If you could change one thing in your life, what would it be?' 'If you were going to be (an animal, a plant, a football team, a drink), what would you be? – Why?'

- ○ Avoid giving advice – this turns most people off. They don't really want to know what you would do, it will just confirm for them that you don't actually understand what they are going through

- ○ Avoid saying 'I know how you feel.' You can't know exactly how they feel, even if you have had similar experiences. Everyone has their own unique experience.

FOR DISCUSSION

Once clients get to know you and understand how you work, they will often reveal more information about their thoughts and feelings related to what you are working on or even reveal a completely unrelated condition that they really want to focus on. This often happens around the third or fourth treatment. What could you do to encourage your clients to feel more relaxed in your company and possibly reveal what is really bothering them earlier?

TASK

Role play

This exercise helps you to understand how difficult it is to remember things that your client has said, to summarise them and to feed them back. It will also show you how difficult many people find it to be positive about themselves. Carry out this exercise without using paper or taking notes. Working in pairs, take it in turns to ask the questions and respond. See how many of your 'client' answers you can remember at the end of the session.

(**a**) *five activities the client enjoys doing*

(**b**) *five events that have happened to the client in the last month*

(**c**) *five skills the client has*

Note: What's the point? You won't always have your notebook out when the client gives you key pieces of information. They may choose to confide in you during the treatment process, at which point you will need to remember what was said to write it down later.

The consultation process

The consultation process is a necessary step that we take prior to treatment. It gives both therapist and client the opportunity to

○ communicate with each other – for the client to talk about the reason for seeking treatment, any expectations they hold of the treatment process and for the therapist to clarify what they can expect of the treatment

○ assess one another – this is usually being done on a non-verbal level, where both client and therapist are determining whether they feel safe and comfortable with the idea of proceeding with treatment

○ check for any contraindications

○ establish the areas to focus on during treatment

○ complete information needed to carry out a treatment safely

○ relax from the journey.

The client's response to the consultation process is likely to vary with the treatment you are carrying out, their expectations of you and their understanding of what is involved. With many body treatments, you can expect that the client is going to want you to hurry through the consultation and get on with the treatment itself, so they may be impatient if you take a lengthy time to carry out the consultation. Take the time to explain the importance of the consultation to the client and you may find their attitude changes (but at the same time, don't take forever to get the information!).

What should appear in your client notes?

Your consultation form and client record cards should contain all the information you need to work effectively in your chosen discipline and to keep accurate records of the treatment process and your client's responses to treatment. A consultation form needs to give you the space to write details about the client's personal circumstances and, where there are presenting conditions, details about how the client experiences these and what makes it better or worse. A checklist of contraindications to treatment is not enough. In an effective consultation sheet, you should find space to write down the following information:

○ client contact details

○ client's doctor's contact details

○ reasons for treatment

○ what makes this better/worse

○ what they have already tried (and whether it worked)

○ medical history (in brief, but usually on a system-by-system basis)

○ diet/intake issues (to include nicotine, alcohol, any prescriptions and the use of any recreational drugs – if they will tell you)

○ stressors – these could include work, family, partners/relationships, or other aspects

○ date and details of each treatment, including client's response before and after treatments

○ any home-care advice given for each treatment.

TASK

Design a set of consultation forms that suit the needs of your treatment process.

Getting the information you need

Once you have explained to your client why you need to fill out the consultation form and set up your records for them, there are certain things you can do to help the client understand why you are asking the questions you do and to help them to focus on what they want to get out of the treatment:

○ Warm them up by establishing contact details first, these are less private than the rest of the information you will require

○ Move on to their reasons for seeking treatment – this is the purpose they are seeing you for and should be seen as a key concern

○ Establish how these reasons are affecting the client physically and emotionally. What makes the condition better or worse? What have they already done to try to handle it?

○ Follow up with questions related to the body systems or habits that are most likely to show symptoms relating to the key reasons for treatment (for instance if they are complaining about stress-related aches and pains you may want to move on to ask about other symptoms that are vulnerable to stress: their diet – particularly caffeine, nicotine and alcohol intake; their bowel movements; their sleeping patterns; blood pressure, and so on)

- ○ Check any contraindications to treatment
- ○ Finish up by asking the client if there is anything else they think you should know about. The line of your questioning may prompt them to add something else.

With the consultation process, it is very important to bear in mind that even the most innocent-sounding questions could potentially be seen as offensive or invasive if asked at the wrong time or in the wrong way. For example, asking a client about the number of children they have could be traumatic if they were experiencing difficulties conceiving, where contemplating adoption or abortion or if the child/children they did have were unwell or in difficulties at the time. Be tactful and considerate at all times.

FOR DISCUSSION

Look at your own consultation sheet. What questions do you think could be viewed as invasive? How could you reword the questions to make them more appropriate to the client's needs and more comfortable for them to answer?

Why keep accurate records?

Although record-keeping is a requirement laid down on therapists by most of the governing bodies, the temptation to avoid doing your paperwork could be huge, especially if you are running a very busy practice and don't have much time between clients.

Keeping records is for your protection as well as for the well-being of your client. In the event of something going wrong – perhaps the client decides to sue you – your records of the treatment process could be used to argue that you were acting appropriately, as long as they are full and complete records that outline what you did in the treatment and why you did it. Things you could expect to include in your treatment notes above and beyond the client's contact details include:

- ○ Nature of the treatment carried out (this is especially important if you practise more than one kind of treatment)
- ○ Areas or issues you concentrated on
- ○ Signs or symptoms specific to the client (for instance areas of greater tension, or where skin colour or texture changes, etc)
- ○ If you noticed anything that you felt needed checking out by the GP, did you tell the client? Did they check it out and report back to you?
- ○ Suggestions you made for home care or after care
- ○ Did you warn them of any possible side effects?
- ○ Reminders to yourself about what you might try next time
- ○ Reminders about issues the client was concerned about

- How the client is responding to treatment, both in the treatment and between treatments. Did they experience any side effects?

- Whether the client has followed your suggestions and, if so, how they are reacting to them

- Any doctor's letters that you received as part of the treatment process, for instance if there was a contraindication to treatment that needed medical permission for treatment to take place.

TASK

Role play

A client comes to you for treatment and, when you go through the consultation process, you discover a number of symptoms that are worrying and which leave you with the impression that you should not treat this person until they have seen a GP and that preferably they should see a GP very soon. How will you get this message across without alarming the client?

Working in pairs, go through your consultation process with one person playing the part of the therapist and the other taking the part of the client.

Conversation during treatment

As you go through the consultation process, you will need to ask some questions of your client in order to establish the parameters for treatment. This process can go some way to developing a strong bond of trust between client and therapist. The client is telling you a great deal about their personal health, both physical and in some cases psychological as well. They need to know that you can be trusted to keep their secrets, that you are empathic – that you have an insight into their thoughts, feelings and conditions and that you are able to listen to them when they need to talk. Once they feel that they can trust you, often more information will come out, sometimes this information can completely change the direction

DEFINITION

Bacteria – a single celled micro-organism. Removing them requires high temperatures and/or strong chemical substances. Common bacteria infections include salmonella poisoning, strep throat, infected acne and boils.

of the treatment or your understanding of how to proceed.

Not every client needs to talk, so often the best way forward for the therapist is to set the stage for conversation during the treatment. You could do this effectively by

○ starting the treatment by letting the client know that it is okay for them to talk or not to talk as they prefer

○ do not talk yourself unless the client starts the conversation and then only converse on the topics they choose to speak of

○ do not offer advice, unless it is relevant home care or after care advice pertaining to the treatment you are practising

○ keep your sentences short and to the point the client has referred to if asked a question. Where possible, direct the question back to the client, so that they are encouraged to talk instead.

Hints and tips for avoiding conversation

There will be times when you feel it is inappropriate to talk during the treatment process or that it is not helping your client to relax or you to concentrate.

This is especially true during some body treatments and energetic work. The following techniques can be useful if you need to take a break from conversation with your client:

○ use gentle music as a background to your treatment. Many clients prefer music as it further relaxes them and they will often start a conversation as the silence can be oppressive

○ lower the lighting in the room you are working in, this can encourage clients to fall asleep during body treatments

○ if you are carrying out a body treatment, start your treatment working on either the head or the back as these sections can be the most relaxing to the client (and it is very difficult to talk whilst face down or having your head worked on!)

○ for other physical treatments, encouraging the client to concentrate on their breathing during the treatment not only improves oxygen delivery to the body, but is also very difficult to do whilst talking

○ if the client really needs to talk about issues that are beyond the scope of your practice, consider referring them to a practitioner who specialises in counselling or similar work.

DEFINITION

Bacteriostat – something that slows down the growth of bacteria.

Contraindications

Contraindications are particular conditions or circumstances that suggest it may be necessary not to treat the client or where you are able to treat the client but should proceed with caution and/or take additional precautions whilst working.

Contraindications should usually be established during the consultation process at the first treatment and, if appropriate, you may need to check the progress of the condition at the start of later treatments.

Contraindications will vary from one form of treatment to another, although they can generally be divided into three categories:

○ Total – usually refers to a condition that makes a standard treatment inadvisable or where treating in your usual fashion could be dangerous for the client. This does not necessarily mean that you should not treat at all, but you may need to take further precautions or, if you are not confident, you may wish to refer the client on to another practitioner or ask them to seek advice from their doctor before coming for treatment.

○ Local – means that something has occurred in a particular area of the body which means that you could treat the rest of the body but you are advised not to work in the area in question.

○ Medical – means that the client has a condition which they are seeing a GP or specialist for. To treat them you must have written permission from the doctor.

TASK

What are the total, local and medical contraindications to the treatment that you practise?

FOR DISCUSSION

How would you deal with a client who comes to you for the first time and appears to have a contraindication to treatment?

Hygiene, health and safety whilst working

Although it is virtually impossible to get or maintain a sterile working environment for a therapist, it is extremely important to keep hygiene levels as high as possible for the safety and comfort of therapist and client. Strict hygiene methods will help to prevent cross infection and disease as well as making the treatment process more comfortable and pleasant for therapist and client alike.

Some of the hygiene methods you should be considering, regardless of whether you work from home, in a salon, health centre, spa or as part of a mobile practice, include the following:

○ Washing of hands with antibacterial/antiseptic substances before and after each treatment

○ When colds or similar are about, remembering to wash your hands after blowing your nose and not coughing or sneezing over your client. Consider using a mask if feasible

○ Have clean, appropriate towels or cloths to wipe your hands on following washing them

○ Keep animals away from the treatment room

○ If carrying out body treatments, use antibacterial wipes (or surgical spirits) to clean the feet prior to treatment, then wash your hands before carrying out the treatment

○ Keep the treatment area properly ventilated (but warm enough for the client)

○ Do not touch your face, hair or another part of your body and then return your hands to the client without washing them first (for body treatments)

○ Use disposable gloves for any treatment that involves piercings, or could bring you into contact with body fluids (for instance electrolysis, waxing, piercings, tattooing, acupuncture, colonic irrigation, etc)

○ Clean towels for every client receiving body treatments

○ Use of couch roll/hygiene roll, provided fresh for each client

○ Removal of all waste substances after each client

○ Disinfecting waste bins daily

○ Appropriate removal of clinical waste (such as electrolysis or acupuncture needles or anything involving blood or bodily fluids)

○ Any needles used are provided in sterile, unopened packaging, which is opened in front of the client for their use only and NEVER recycled

○ Floors mopped with disinfectants on a daily basis

○ All toilet and washing facilities thoroughly scrubbed with disinfectants (antibacterial and antiseptic) on a daily basis

○ Sterilisation of equipment where possible and used appropriately.

FOR DISCUSSION

What other methods could you take to ensure high levels of hygiene in your workplace?

DEFINITION

Cross infection – passing an infection from one area of the body to another or from one person to another. Adequate hygiene methods are used to avoid cross infection.

Safety

Keeping your treatment space and process safe and free from danger means that you need to be observant about potential hazards to yourself and the client. Revisit the legislation relating to health and safety at work, manual handling, electricity at work and the workplace regulations as well as considering carrying out the following on a regular basis:

○ check that any couch or treatment equipment is safe to use and properly assembled

○ help the client onto and off any equipment, providing steps or a hydraulic couch if possible (for body treatments)

○ ensure that all the client's belongings are safely stored out of the way, so that you don't trip over them whilst working

○ keep any products or items used during the treatment out of the way (perhaps using a trolley or a table nearby), so that you don't spill them during the treatment

○ keep the floor clean and free of obstacles

○ clean up any spillages immediately, so that slipping is avoided

○ wear non-slip shoes with a good tread to avoid slipping

○ keep the client properly covered and warm during treatment

○ provide clean towels and hygiene rolls for each client

○ ensure that you have taken your personal safety into account

○ try not to leave the client in the treatment room alone, in case something happens (such as a fall), this is especially important if you know they have a serious medical condition where sudden changes are possible – such as epilepsy.

The importance of hygiene and sterilisation

Maintaining high levels of hygiene and taking the time to sterilise equipment is vitally important given the ease with which bacteria, viruses or fungi can get into the human body and bring on disease. There are three ways that access is possible:

○ inhalation

○ ingestion

○ through gaps in the body's existing defences.

DEFINITION

Disinfectant – will kill bacteria but is usually too strong to be used on the skin.

DEFINITION

Natural or innate immunity – *these are the methods the body employs to reduce the risk of infection from any source. These methods include enzymes found in tears and saliva, which destroy bacteria; hairs and mucus in the nose to prevent the entry of dust and micro-organisms; sneezing; mucus and cilia in the respiratory and digestive tracts, which trap foreign particles; hydrochloric acid in the stomach to destroy micro-organisms; beneficial bacteria in the intestines control harmful organisms; sebaceous glands in the skin secreting chemicals toxic to most bacteria; inflammation, which causes redness, pain, heat and swelling but also traps microbes, toxins and foreign material at the site of injury and prepares the body for repair. Innate methods of immunity are not affected by the action of lymphocytes.*

FOR DISCUSSION

Given the body's natural methods of maintaining immunity, what do you think are the most likely ways that a bacterium could get in to the body? What methods of hygiene do you use as a therapist to reduce the risk of this happening?

FOR REFLECTION

Think back to your understanding of the digestive system and the respiratory system. What mechanisms exist to prevent or reduce the risk of infection entering the body via these systems?

Methods of sterilising equipment

Radiation

Ultra-violet – used in small cabinets. Only appropriate if storing equipment that is already clean. Best used alongside another form of sterilisation.

Heat

Dry – items should be clean first and able to withstand extremely high temperatures. Can use hot air ovens for large equipment or a glass bead steriliser for small metal items.

Moist – boiling for five minutes or longer will destroy most kinds of bacteria, infestations, spores or viruses. Hence the need to boil wash any towels or laundry. Autoclaves will increase pressure and temperature of boiling water so can destroy all organisms. Dishwashers, whilst reasonably effective, are unable to remove all bacteria or viruses.

Chemicals

Ideal for cleaning surfaces and most materials. Always read the label to determine the most appropriate chemicals for the use you intend. Examples will include bleach, most disinfectants, hydrogen peroxide etc.

Knowing when to refer on

There will be times when you feel it is appropriate to refer your client on to either their GP, a physiotherapist, a medical specialist or to another complementary therapist. As part of your professional code of ethics and behaviour it will be necessary at times to admit that you may be out of your depth emotionally, mentally or physically where a client is concerned. Referring someone on is not an admission of failure, quite the opposite; it shows that you recognise where your skills begin and end. You may choose to refer on in one or more of the following circumstances:

○   you suspect a serious, but undiagnosed, condition

○   the client is worried about a condition or symptom and hasn't yet been to the doctor

○   the client is not responding to your treatment

○   key contraindications preclude treatment

○   you do not feel safe with the client

○   they cross your personal boundaries – either through a clash of personalities or you are too involved with their emotions or interests to treat them objectively.

DEFINITION

Fungistat – something that slows down the growth or spreading of fungal infections.

Who to refer on to?

Networking with other therapists will help you to learn more about the industry in which you work, give you ideas for any additional courses you might some day wish to take and which can potentially bring you increased business. For a serious medical condition, or where there are worrying signs or symptoms your first recommendation should be that the client seeks advice from their GP. However, if your client is not responding to your treatment, you may wish to suggest one of the following. Make sure that they do not conflict in nature with the work that you do with the client, or if they are likely to, ensure that the client is aware of any potential symptoms before they happen.

Complementary Therapy	Brief Description
Acupuncture	Aims to restore the balance of the bodily energy or life force (Qi) where it has been disrupted, to relieve pain and restore health. Acupuncture is sometimes seen as part of Traditional Chinese Medicine. Very fine (sterilised) needles are inserted into the skin at acupressure (or meridian) points and are left there for up to 30 minutes at a time to get the desired results.
Alexander Technique	Teaches a new way of thinking about and using the body in order to eliminate unconscious habits of tension, particularly those that constrict the spine. The improvement in posture, moving, walking and breathing can result in general health improvements.
Aromatherapy	The use of essential oils, distillations of the leaves, flowers, bark, seeds or resins of plants, in order to improve or enhance health and well-being. The essential oils are usually administered via body massage, although they can also be applied via inhalations, vaporisers, hot or cold compresses and various bathing products.
Bach Flower Remedies	The remedies are taken from wild plants, bushes and trees and placed in a bowl filled with spring water. The plant material 'potentises' the water, imprinting it with its essences. These remedies are used to harmonise emotional imbalances.
Bowen Technique	Similar to Kinesiology in that practitioners believe that meridians or energy lines exist between muscles and internal organs as well as the emotions of the client. Minute adjustments made to the client's muscles (after which the client is left to relax into the change before the next set of adjustments is made) result in more profound changes on the emotional and physical levels.
Chiropractic	Chiropractors diagnose by feeling (or palpating) and treat disorders of the spine, joints and muscles by manual adjustment, often with the help of X-rays. They aim to improve function, relieve pain and increase mobility. Their main focus is the spinal vertebrae although their manipulations can relieve conditions that are not musculoskeletal in origin.

Complementary Therapy	Brief Description
Herbalism	Uses plant remedies in the treatment of disease and for ensuring health and well-being. Treatment is holistic with each person being treated as unique. Herbalists look for the cause of illness, rather than treating the symptoms and attribute disease to a disruption in the body's state of harmony or homeostasis.
Homeopathy	Based on the theory that 'like cures like' (so whatever made you sick will be used to cure you) and the principle of the minimum dose – the active ingredient is diluted many times before being used to treat a client. The remedy is believed to stimulate the body's immune system and strengthen it against all illnesses, not just the one being treated.
Iridology	A diagnostic technique that uses changes in the appearance of the eye, particularly the iris, to indicate changes or weaknesses in the physical body, usually before they manifest. The eyes are used to assess the state of health and well-being by looking at the condition, pigmentation, structure and markings of the iris.
Kinesiology	Based on the idea that there are meridians that connect all body organs and muscles. Weaknesses in specific muscles indicate potential illnesses or help to diagnose existing imbalances. Weak muscles indicate problem areas, which the therapist then treats by gently massaging appropriate acupressure points on the body or scalp. This revitalises the flow of energy.
Osteopathy	A holistic system of diagnosis and treatment that focuses on structural and mechanical problems of the musculoskeletal system. Osteopathy aims to correct these problems and reduce the likelihood of problems recurring.
Physiotherapy	Concentrates on remedial massage and rehabilitation of individuals following injury or disease. Physiotherapists use a range of manipulative techniques common to osteopathy and chiropractic as well as other forms of mechanical massage and exercises in order to improve the rate of recovery in their clients. They are regarded as the most acceptable form of complementary therapy by the majority of medics and work extensively within the health service.
Reflexology	Acupressure massage of the feet. Practitioners believe that the feet reflect the condition of specific parts of the body with the left foot representing areas and organs on the left side of the body and so on. The treatment also clears energy blockages present in these areas that may be responsible for physical problems or emotional upsets.
Reiki/Spiritual Healing	A hands-on healing system for channelling life force. The practitioner acts as a channel for healing energy. These therapies are particularly useful for eliminating stress and inducing a feeling of relaxation and well-being. Profound physical changes have been noticed in some individuals as well. The key difference between the two methods involves the way in which the therapist focusses their attention and the energy on the client.
Shiatsu	A Japanese acupressure massage technique that encourages the steady flow of Qi energy, correcting imbalances to health through firm pressures to particular points along the body and scalp.
Yoga/Meditation	A method of training the body, mind and spirit that emphasises awareness and control of both body and mind through a series of physical postures known as asanas, which can be performed standing, kneeling, sitting or lying. All movements emphasise breath control, suppleness and flexibility of limbs, joints and spine.

TASK

What therapists are practising within your local area? Develop a list of potential people you could refer clients to should they require a different form of treatment.

Signs and symptoms of disease

When you are going through the consultation process with your client, whilst you will be checking for the specific contraindications to your treatment, clients can occasionally mention certain signs or symptoms that they are worried about but which they can't connect to anything that they know of themselves or that has been diagnosed for them. Remember that only medical practitioners have the experience and knowledge to diagnose conditions.

To protect your client's interests (and your own), politely but firmly suggest a trip to the GP if you see or suspect any of the following signs. Although they don't necessarily mean that something serious is happening, it is better to check the situation out than to risk making things worse by ignoring it:

○ Weight loss without dieting

○ Loss of appetite for no apparent reason

○ Sudden weight gain, despite dieting, especially when only in one area

DEFINITION

Non-pathogenic – something that is not disease causing.

DEFINITION

Pathogenic – disease-causing substance or micro-organism.

- Extreme temperature changes – very hot or cold, night sweats
- Unexplained vomiting
- Difficulty breathing, swallowing or talking
- Unexplained blood loss from any orifice
- Excessive or prolonged bleeding in menstruation
- Unidentified lumps and bumps that have not been investigated
- Moles, skin tags or lumps and bumps that are increasing in size, changing colour or shape
- Pain – especially if it is continuous, long-lasting and isn't affected by changing position
- Lethargy, weakness and tiredness – especially if it has been going on for a long time. This can relate to a number of conditions, so ask more questions from your client about it. How long has it been going on for? What happened to them about the time it started? Does anything make it better or worse?
- Unusual colour to the skin – cyanosed (or blue) lips, cheeks, palms; if they appear very pale, grey, jaundiced (yellowish, especially around the eyes) or very red (in the face, the palms or as a result of a rash).

DEFINITION

Septic – a surface or area that is infected or where bacteria, fungi, toxins or viruses are present.

DEFINITION

Sterile – a surface that is free from infection and all micro-organisms.

Lesley Bacon is European Area Manager for Esporta health clubs, a former General Manager for Esporta and former Club Manager for Mark Warner's summer and winter all-inclusive hotels. In all of these roles she has been involved in recruiting and interviewing beauty and complementary health professionals to work within the clubs in a salon environment.

❝ *Yes I do have certain expectations when I am hiring a new therapist or a team of therapists. I expect them to look immaculate and to appear as if they practise what they preach, which means they must look as if they take care of their own health too. I would expect them to be quite friendly and personable. This doesn't mean that they need to be oozing self-confidence in the interview, but they should appear at ease. Given the job they are applying to do, I would expect to enjoy talking to them; someone interested in health and well-being tends to be a very positive person to have around.*

I will usually have seen their curriculum vitae before the interview, so I will know the basics of what the person has achieved and is interested in, but I do expect someone to be able to talk me through their experiences, as most people don't do themselves justice when putting together a written CV. What I will do is use the CV to see if someone matches the job description with their experiences and qualifications. The interview will then give me an idea as to whether their personality fits into the job and environment and whether I think they will be able to reflect the company's values.

continued...

I tend to ask questions that relate to the work they do, for example, I might ask them what therapies they would recommend I try, or which treatments (if they do more than one) they prefer doing and why. If I am interviewing a male therapist, I will be interested in asking why they went into this work, as on average about 90% of the therapists who approach us for work are female.

The rest of the interview questions tend to focus on the level of commercial understanding the therapist has – are they aware of how many treatments they will need to do and how many hours they will need to work in order to be paid the salary offered? I would also expect them to show their understanding of and commitment to getting and maintaining repeat business. Treatments are not essential purchases to the client so the therapist must be offering an exceptional experience that will make them part with their money and decide that it was so good they need to come back.

If I am recruiting for a new club, one that is just opening, then the therapist's commercial understanding becomes even more important, as they will need to be far more closely involved with attracting business to the salon. Whilst it is easier to launch the health club first and then launch the salon at a later date as an added benefit to members (and you then have a captive audience) this is not always possible. New therapists working in the health club need to be prepared to go out and talk to members in the café, the reception area, the crèche, and everywhere else to creatively promote themselves and their services.

continued...

I like to see therapists ask me a few questions in the interview. Not only does it show that they are undaunted by the interview process, but it also shows that they are interested in the company and in the job. This doesn't mean they have to remember the questions, having them written down in advance is absolutely fine. I do expect them to look up the company or do a little research into the people they will be interviewed by, as this shows that their commitment to their work goes beyond a desire just to pay the bills into something more substantial.

I suppose the best advice I can give to someone going for an interview is to turn up early. Even if this means you are sitting in the café waiting for a bit before they are ready for you, it is far better than being late. Aim to appear confident, friendly and personable – this is not a job for loners! Whilst we will need to check certificates and do a trade test, these don't usually occur during the first interview. If you are applying to work in a health centre, you do need to have an interest in health and fitness, although you don't have to be a fitness guru – just as long as you have an outgoing personality and can take an active interest in the other services offered by the club. There are often opportunities for the therapists to promote these services during a treatment, and to sell effectively you need to be enthusiastic and knowledgeable.

continued...

That ability to promote themselves and their work effectively is actually very important, even if a therapist doesn't choose to work in a spa or salon. People don't try a new therapist easily or readily, especially if they already have someone they trust. To get them to try someone new takes a very special kind of person and an excellent treatment. I've noticed that people don't really move on price alone. A cheaper price isn't going to set the world on fire. You don't have to undercut all your competitors, just make sure that you give your clients an extremely good service. For example, if you are charging £25 for a treatment, they should feel as if they got £30 worth at least. Undercutting everyone else on price may be a good idea initially, but be careful you aren't selling yourself short; keep your price close to everyone else's or you may find that clients start to question the quality of the treatment you are offering. **"**

DEFINITION

Sterilisation – the complete removal of living micro-organisms. In most cases, it is impossible completely to sterilise a therapist's working conditions or equipment, hence the need to maintain hygiene levels at all times.

Checking your understanding

1. Why do you feel it is important for a therapist to observe a professional code of ethics?

2. Explain what is meant by professional ethics

3. Explain what is meant by client care and modesty. How can you effectively support these in your practice?

4. Why is personal hygiene important to the therapist?

5. What steps would you take to maintain hygiene in the clinic?

6. Outline the advantages and disadvantages of the different methods of sterilisation. Which methods are most practical for you to use in your own work?

7. Why is it important to maintain clear, accurate records?

8. What case history would you take prior to giving a new client a treatment?

9. Explain, with examples, the differences between total, local and medical contraindications

10. List all the contraindications to your treatment

11. What signs and symptoms would you look for that might indicate potential dangers to the client?

12. When would you refer a client to another practitioner or GP?

DEFINITION

Toxins – substances produced by a disease-causing organism. These will often produce side effects of their own (like fever or inflammation).

Viruses – small, disease-causing micro-organisms that will live inside human cells and are extremely resistant to removal. The client's response to the presence of the virus will vary according to the virus and the condition of the client's immune system. Vaccinations have been developed in part to reduce the effects of many serious and potentially lethal viruses, such as smallpox, typhoid fever, cholera, hepatitis, rubella or measles. Examples of other viruses include HIV, chicken pox, warts, cold sores and the common cold.

10 Managing your aspirations

Objectives

At the end of this chapter, you should be able to

O Draw up a curriculum vitae (CV) and covering letter

O Present yourself effectively at interview

O Describe what is meant by the product life cycle

O Describe what is meant by the Boston Matrix

O Explain how these two terms apply to your business

O Understand what preparations need to be made in order to run a workshop effectively

O Make suggestions for how you can promote your business after its initial launch

Introduction

Once you have developed your business vision, produced a plan and marketing material, identified your clients and made every effort to make your business as efficient and effective as possible, the key ingredient still remains to be considered: you. This business has to work for you, it should inspire you, keep you enthusiastic and give you a clear sense of where you are going and how you want to get there. This chapter concentrates on things you can do to keep your business going and to help you exploit every possible opportunity available to you. It also gives you an idea of the signs to look for to indicate when it might be time to alter the focus of your marketing or the focus of your business.

Drawing up a curriculum vitae

One of the most useful things you can produce for your business is your curriculum vitae (CV), sometimes called a resumé. This will be necessary for most jobs that you apply for, although some companies will have an application form that they wish you to fill in. It gives prospective employers a brief insight into your interests and experiences and helps them to make sure that you have all the requirements they are looking for when considering hiring you. They will be checking your CV before they interview you to make sure that they are not wasting your time – or theirs – by calling you for interview. As such, your CV has an important role to play in attracting enough interest to encourage your prospective employer to at least talk to you. Think of it as an advert for you.

There are a few conventions as to what makes an effective CV:

O Clearly laid out and legible

O Typed or word-processed

O All spelling and punctuation are correct

O No longer than two sides of A4 paper

O Printed on good quality paper

○ Contains the following details in this order:

  ○ your contact details

  ○ educational qualifications (you do not need to list your earliest qualifications in detail unless specifically asked for them)

  ○ work experience/career and achievements

  ○ interests and hobbies

  ○ at least two references – one personal and one professional. If you are just leaving college, the professional one could be your tutor.

○ It may contain a statement from you as to your personal aims and objectives, but this is optional

○ When you describe your work experience, include the job title and key responsibilities of the job and you could also include key achievements related to that job

○ When outlining your career and achievements, put the most recent ones first and work backwards from there

○ For your educational and any academic or post-qualification training, start with your earliest training and work forwards from there.

TASK

Task: Produce your own CV following the guidelines above. You may find the illustration provided useful.

CURRICULUM VITAE

Name:	Anne Other
Date of birth:	07.09.80
Address:	72 Any Road, Anytown, Herts, HRS QSZ
Telephone no:	. . . .
Marital status:	Single
Car driver:	Full licence
School/further education	Peaks Comprehensive Natler Road Anytown September 1991 – July 1998 Anytown FE College, Anytown September 1998 – July 2000

Examinations: June 1998	GCSE	Passes	Grade
	English Language		A
	English Literature		B
	French		B
	History		A
	Biology		B
	Physics		C
	Art		B
	'A' Level		
	English		B

July 2000	City and Guilds Certificate in Beauty Therapy Certificate in Electrolysis
Work experience:	Debenhams Department Store Anytown Two weeks April 1998
Interest/hobbies:	Swimming, reading, dancing
References:	Mrs R Scott, Head Teacher, Peaks Comprehensive School, Anytown (former head teacher) Mr P Maitland, The Manager Debenhams Department Store, Anytown (former employer)

Figure 10.1 A sample CV

The covering letter

Regardless of whether you are asked to fill in an application form or produce a CV, a covering letter is a vital part of any job application. This works almost like the leaflet for your business. Where the CV is the bare bones of who you are and what you do, the covering letter gives you a chance to expand on that, and tell your prospective employer why you are the perfect person for the job they have available. An effective covering letter will do the following:

○ address the person who is advertising the post

○ if you heard about the post through someone, mention their name in the first paragraph

○ if you heard about the post through a newspaper (or magazine), say which newspaper and on what date

○ make connections between the advertisement you saw (or any information you received about the job) and your own experiences. For instance, if your prospective employer is looking for someone with experience or an understanding of sports-related injuries, then you could mention any relevant practice or qualifications or your own involvement and interest in specific sports

○ tell them why you want the job. Try to leave out 'for the salary' as this does not inspire confidence! A more appropriate answer could include references to the kinds of working experience you might gain or access to specific client groups or even the support they offer new therapists as part of any training programme. If the hours that you would be working are important to you, or an attraction of the job, this is also acceptable

○ remind them of your contact details and let them know when you are available for interview.

A new complementary health centre and spa is opening up in your local area. They have advertised for therapists and say they are looking for 'professional, experienced individuals with a commitment to health in general and strong proven interests in working with stress-related conditions.' They offer a choice of full- or part-time positions. Write a covering letter to go with your CV, applying for a position.

Presenting yourself for interview

If your application proves successful, you may be asked to attend an interview with your prospective employer. These interviews can vary with the employer and with the discipline you are practising. For the most part, it is safe to assume that part of the interview process will involve you carrying out part, or all, of a treatment under observation. Although the employer will be able to see what qualifications you hold from your CV, there is still quite a lot of variation between the different qualifications available, so they will want to have a good idea of just what they are getting in a prospective employee. They also want to get an idea as to who you are and what you are like as a person. Not only do they want to get the best therapists possible, but they also want to know that you fit in with the other members of their team. To present yourself effectively for interview, consider doing the following:

○ Make sure your appearance is immaculate and professional. If you know you are to carry out a treatment, you may wish to bring a uniform with you to change into.

○ Arrive a little early for the interview, so that you have time to catch your breath and calm down before the session takes place.

○ If you are to carry out a treatment, check that all the equipment you will need is going to be available, otherwise take your own.

○ Check with your prospective employer to find out if they will need to see anything else from you at the interview stage – will they want copies of your certificates, for instance?

○ Read through any information you can find about the company in advance of the interview. A popular interview question is 'what do you know about this company?' Most larger companies have a website, so this could be your first source of information.

○ Remember to make eye contact with your interviewer and smile as appropriate.

○ Watch your own body language, so that it suggests that you are confident and assured. If you are very nervous or your hands tend to shake, keep them folded and in your lap. Avoid crossing your arms over your body, hunching forward or tapping your feet excessively. These are just some of the signs that indicate you are nervous or tense.

○ Take your time answering their questions so that you consider exactly what you are saying, then say it without hesitating. This is especially important if you tend to speed up when you are nervous. You may feel you are taking a long time to answer, but you probably aren't.

- ⭕ Try to link their questions to your own experiences where possible. They are asking those questions to give you a chance to talk so they can get to know you.

- ⭕ Before you go to the interview, take time to think about the kinds of question they might ask and how you would answer them. This will make you feel less nervous and help you to develop more complete answers to the questions.

- ⭕ If you are given the chance to ask questions, make sure these are relevant to the interview and suggest that you are interested in the job. You could prepare these questions in advance.

TASK

Working in pairs or in groups of three, select one person to be the interviewee and one or two people to be the interviewers. The interviewers should draw up a list of questions they want the interviewee to answer during the interview in advance. Role play the interview – and be as tough on the interviewee as you like. Provide feedback on how well you think they did, using the key points listed above. Remember that practising interview techniques now will make the real thing much easier to deal with.

Taking the business further

There comes a point when it is necessary to change what you are doing in order to help your business grow and develop, to stay competitive and still make a profit. Being successful involves anticipating when that time has come as well as recognising where you and your business stand in relation to all the other therapists out there.

There are two key concepts that can help you to work out where you stand in the market place and to suggest what to try next to make things work for you. These are

- ⭕ the product life cycle – which helps you look at the stage your treatment and business are at

- ⭕ the Boston Matrix – which helps you compare your rate of growth with your market share.

The product life cycle

Interest in a product or service changes with time, and with this change in interest you will also see changes to

- ⭕ the costs you have to pay to promote your services effectively

- ⭕ the number of competitors you face

- ⭕ the kinds of client that come for treatment

- ⭕ the kinds of marketing effort you need to make

- ⭕ the prices you can charge

- ⭕ the kind of product you can offer to attract those clients.

Recognising that every product or service goes through these different stages – introduction, growth, maturity and decline – can help you to decide where you fit on the scale, the kinds of problem you are likely to encounter and what your best approach is going to be to tackle what you face. One important factor to consider when looking at the product life cycle is that this refers not only to your services as a therapist, but also to the whole complementary therapies and beauty industry in your area. Ask yourself how familiar people are with the kind of service you offer? Have they heard of your treatment process before? In either case you might place your product or service in the growth, maturity or decline sections (and hopefully your share of the business is growing faster and more profitably than others). Is it completely new to them? In which case it belongs in the introductory section.

In practice, the product life cycle can give us an insight into what to expect in the following areas.

Clients

The product life cycle divides clients into four categories based on how and when they decide to try your services. **Innovators** are the first people to try anything. They tend to be keen, enthusiastic, well informed and willing to try new things. Innovators will be the clients who put a lot of effort into tracking you down if you have a new product or service; will be very aware of what other services are available (and may well have tried them all); and will also have an active commitment to their own health and well-being. You could expect to find a lot of other therapists in this group.

The **early majority**, or **early adopters**, will be the second wave of clients that you see. These groups are reasonably committed to their own health, less well informed than the innovators, but quite aware of what is going on around them. They will be responding to your promotional efforts and to what they hear about your services from other people. This is the group that you want to attract as soon as possible as your business will often increase dramatically when they arrive and your profit line will look far healthier.

The **late majority**, or **late adopters**, arrive when your business or the product you offer has been around for a while and has become established. They might not personally understand how and why the treatment works, but they have been aware of it for some time and have heard about it from friends, families, colleagues or similar.

The **laggards** are the last people to try the treatment and may even be doing so under some duress. They may be unconvinced of any benefits to be obtained from complementary treatments.

Competitors

In the introductory phase, there will be only a few competitors, these increase in the growth phase, with a lot of competitors in the maturity phase and fewer in the decline phase.

Pricing

In the introductory phase you can get away with charging high prices because your treatment process is new, prices need to drop as you go into the growth phase, will reach their lowest point during the maturity phase and can rise again slightly in the decline phase (because there are fewer competitors at this time). Note that this does not mean that you can charge a lot when you first qualify! If you are working in a discipline where there are a lot of other therapists working nearby, you need to be as competitive as possible on price.

Product

Your product or service can be very simple and easy to explain during the introduction phase (as it is a new concept that you are offering your clients). You may even need to explain the treatment in terms of something the potential clients are already familiar with, as they may not understand what you are offering if your treatment is complex. In the growth phase you need to make improvements to the product, dealing with any problems that clients might perceive as awkward about the product or service. In the maturity stage you would benefit from making sure that what you offer is noticeably different from all the other therapists offering similar treatments in your area (think back to your unique selling points), and in the decline phase you may be reducing the range of treatments that you offer so that you only offer what is popular and makes you a profit.

Marketing efforts

In the growth phase your marketing efforts will concentrate on providing an information service explaining how your treatment process works and why and what benefits are available to your clients. This will involve quite a lot of effort to convince the innovators and early majority clients to try it out. In the growth phase, you may be involved in convincing would-be clients that the treatment you offer is going to be more effective at meeting their needs than what they are currently doing (whether their current efforts involve 'nothing', or other forms of treatment). In the maturity phase it is advisable that you concentrate on encouraging your clients to remain loyal to you and the service you offer. In the decline phase you may well be very selective about what marketing you carry out and only do that which gives you clear results.

For example

Interest in complementary therapies in general is growing. More GPs are recommending clients to complementary therapists. More research is being done to establish just how effective therapies are in treating specific conditions as well as in supporting clients' emotional well-being. However, where do the various therapies fit in the product life cycle in general?

Let's take Aromatherapy for example. In its current format – as a discipline that involves applying essential oils to the client either as part of a massage or through inhalations, compresses, bathing products or similar – it was first introduced to the United Kingdom (UK) in the 1960s. Today, 40-plus years later, essential oils are widely available, as is information on their use; some of this information has reached even those people who are not interested in Massage or Aromatherapy. As a test, ask your friends or family (those who don't know much about aromatherapy) what tea tree or lavender might be used for. There also appears to be an assumption with many clients that anyone practising therapeutic massage would also be an Aromatherapist, which suggests that a lot of people already know what to expect about the treatment process. Access to Aromatherapy, certainly in the UK, is generally easily available. This might suggest that aromatherapy is somewhere in the growth/maturity section of the product life cycle in the UK. As a result, individual therapists are looking at ways to differentiate their services from other therapists and are keeping prices competitive. An indication that it was going into decline would be if the number of new clients started to drop away and if interest in training courses in Aromatherapy also started to decline.

DISCUSSION

Where do you think Indian Head Massage falls in the product life cycle? To help you decide, consider when you first heard about it, in what context, how many therapists you know who are practising it, how easy it is to find a course in Indian Head Massage and what the therapists you know say about how easy it is to get and keep clients.

The product life cycle in practice

Different products or services grow, peak and decline at different rates. One other way of using the product life cycle is that, after you have worked out what stage your product or business is at, you may wish to consider introducing other elements to expand your business, for instance:

○ introduce a new product to your existing clients (maybe a new treatment or a new service you offer)

○ introduce your existing product to a new market (adapt it to make it appropriate to the new market OR keep it exactly the same)

○ enter a new market with a new product – the riskiest version, make sure you do your research beforehand!

The Boston Matrix

Developed by the Boston Consulting Group, the Boston Matrix is a way of categorising any available product or service in terms of its market share (how many of all the potential customers use its service – the percentage of all the customers available) and its growth (how many new customers are coming to use it – the rate at which it appears to be growing). Products or services that have a high market share, and are continuing to grow in popularity are called 'stars' (for instance, the Harry Potter series would be considered a star product). Services that have a high market share, but aren't growing much are called 'cash cows' (so if you were the only acupuncturist within 20 miles, everybody knew about your services and pretty much anyone who was going to try acupuncture was already visiting you, your business

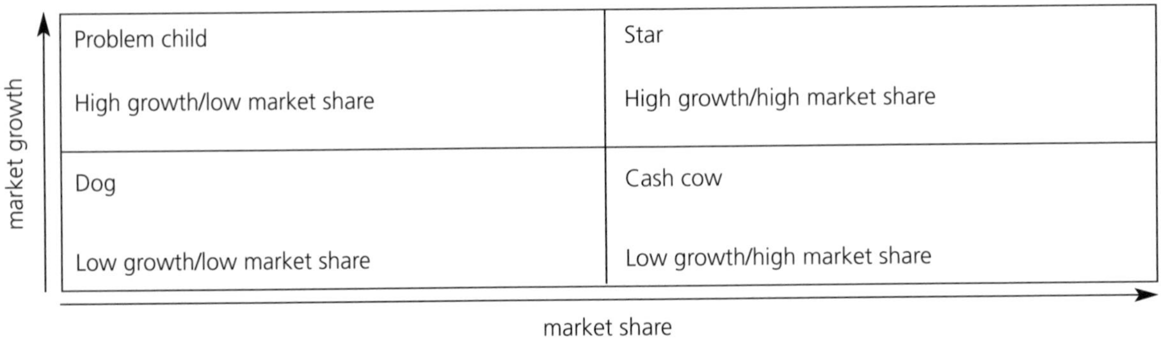

market growth	Problem child High growth/low market share	Star High growth/high market share
	Dog Low growth/low market share	Cash cow Low growth/high market share

market share

Figure 10.2 The Boston Matrix

would be a 'cash cow' business). 'Problem children' are those products or services where you have a low market share but growth is still occurring, whereas 'dogs' are products or services where you have both low market share and low growth.

Unfortunately, most therapists working as individuals on their own will tell you that, for the first few years of their business, their work could be classed as either a 'dog' or a 'problem child', depending on where they are working and how much effort they put into promoting themselves. They will also tell you that different products or services they offer appear to be more popular than others (so for instance a therapist offering more than one kind of treatment will find that treatment x is more popular than treatment y with their clients). The first few years of your business are the toughest ones, as you try out new ideas and find what works best for you and your clients.

In larger businesses, the management will usually try to have a range of different products or services that fall into these categories, so that their business remains healthy over time, continues to grow and always aims to meet the needs of their clients. 'Cash cows', for instance, usually don't need a lot of additional effort spent on them, as they will continue to provide you with an income whilst you concentrate on other areas of the business; you can get away with just doing the minimum required to keep it ticking over. However, the 'cash cows' don't give you much potential for new growth, so whilst they provide plenty of cash in the short term, a sudden change in market conditions could wipe them out. 'Stars' can help you tap into a new outlet or market, although they tend to require quite a bit of promotional activity and a lot of attention so that they remain stable in their growth. With 'stars' you can run the risk of their growing too far too fast so that you could become unable to manage them. They keep your name and services fresh in the public eye. 'Problem children' require a lot of support, encouragement, energy and promotional activity. They have the potential to become 'stars' or 'cash cows', if properly nurtured. Without proper nurturing, they can become 'dogs' and may even be a drain on your expenses. If you have a 'dog' on your hands, it means you need to revisit your marketing strategy and look again at both the promotion you are carrying out and the product or service you are offering.

Finding out which category your business, product or service falls into can help you to decide what kind of action you need to take in order to make things more successful. Some of your choices might include:

Problem child	**Star**
○ Invest in promotion	○ The business is on the increase, work out which promotional activities were most successful and concentrate on keeping those going
○ Try all kinds of promotional activities that are appropriate to your market and do not give up	○ Increase ways of keeping your business in the public eye, especially with your desired clients, possibly using additional, eye-catching promotional material, or getting involved in running workshops, demonstrations or similar that are appealing to your clients
○ Build on the number of new clients you are receiving – try different marketing messages to appeal to different interests or experiences with your clients	
○ Consider ways of getting your clients to bring other new clients for treatment – special offers or discounts to them when they get someone else to book	○ Consider ways of getting your clients to become regulars, either through opportunities to book groups of treatments, special offers or similar

Dog	**Cash cow**
○ Usually arises either at the start of a business when you haven't promoted your work effectively (or at all), at the end of a business's life when interest in the product or service is no longer there or when you have not identified the real needs and desires of your clients (and the product or service doesn't suit them)	○ Leave well enough alone – whatever you are doing is working
	○ Build on the rapport you have with your existing clients, maybe running special events for them or providing an information service
○ Involves a decision – to persevere or to cut your losses and get out	○ Watch closely for changes in market requirements to make sure nothing threatens your position
○ To persevere, revisit your SWOT analysis and check that you have correctly identified all aspects	○ If this has been going for some time, consider introducing another product or service (which may be a problem child or potential star) that anticipates future needs of your clients or taps into a different group of clients for you
○ Revisit your critical success factors and check that you have not left anything out of this list either	
○ Revisit your market research (or conduct new research) to find out what your clients' real needs and desires are	○ Find another group of clients (assuming you have the time!) and introduce your services to them
○ Consider re-launching the product, service or business to the whole client group, but make it look different and make sure your promotional material clearly identifies the clients' actual needs and desires	
○ Consider introducing the service to a new group of clients – perhaps there is another market that you are better able to serve	

A quick way of working out which category your products or services fall into involves working your way through this grid:

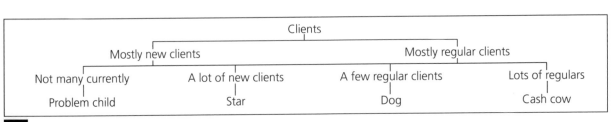

However, bear in mind that a more accurate picture would involve a couple of mathematical equations:

Number of actual clients

Potential number of clients x 100 =

Percentage of market share

Number of new clients

Number of actual clients x 100 =

Percentage of market growth

Applying the Boston Matrix to your business

Question 1: Which category would you put your business into now?

Question 2: What steps could you take to move your business to another category?

Question 3: How would you know when you have moved into another category?

Question 4: What factors could limit your success at making your services either a star or a cash cow business?

Question 5: Are there certain products or services you offer that are more popular than others? Could these be classed as 'cash cows' or 'stars'?

Question 6: What did you do to make your most popular products or services successful? How could you apply this to the rest of your products or services?

Question 7: If you are currently only offering one product or service, how could you vary what you currently offer without engaging in additional training?

Question 8: If you think that your product or service is really a 'dog', why is it a 'dog'? Revisit your SWOT analysis for possible answers.

Post-launch promotion

An area that is often neglected is the promotion that you engage in after your initial launch period. A lot of newly qualified therapists are very good about promoting themselves for the first six months to a year, after which things can tail off. Whilst word-of-mouth promotion is the most effective format, you still need to do some additional work to keep people interested in your work. You can recognise that you are in the post-launch period when you have

○ set up most of your systems

○ a regular group of clients or pattern of working

○ fewer new clients than you did at the beginning (more are now regulars).

At this time you can begin to consider altering the focus of your work or your promotion slightly. Some of your options could include:

○ finding additional venues to work from

○ changing your promotion, perhaps to include seasonal offers or to highlight treatments for specific conditions of interest to your client group

○ trying working in a different way – for instance doing mobile treatments as well as working in a salon

○ promoting to a different group of clients

○ introducing products related to your business and selling these through your existing clients or venues

○ running workshops or demonstrations based around your chosen subject possibly to educate other interested people, to attract new clients or both.

DISCUSSION

What other things could you consider when changing the focus of your work in the post-launch period?

With each of these options, keeping yourself motivated to try new things and persevere with your business is the key to success. Remember that, as with exams, doing the easy questions first (or taking the easy option) is often a good idea to help build your confidence and increase your existing client base first. Investing time and effort in producing new promotional items is often the easiest thing to do in the post-launch period. This will allow you still to focus on your preferred groups of clients and concentrate on attracting their attention with different, possibly more effective, messages.

Selling products can also help to increase the profit that you make from your business. However, it is important to keep a close eye on your cash flow. There may be times when you need to ensure that you only have a limited amount of products and that these sell quickly so that the time and effort you put into promoting the products is of benefit to your business.

Additional venues can open you up to a whole new range of clients, and may be the impetus you need to work towards attracting a new clients, possibly those living in a different area as well as those with different needs and interests.

Turning to training, teaching and workshops

Teaching, running workshops and demonstrations or similar activities is a step that many therapists choose to take as their careers develop, although it is not something that everyone enjoys doing. Teaching itself can be personally and professionally rewarding as it gives you a chance to pass on your love and enthusiasm for your subject to others, as well as giving them the benefit of your experience, regardless of whether you are teaching introductory courses, one-day workshops, taking your students up to practitioner level or beyond.

Running workshops or demonstrations can be very useful, as they provide more information about your business to potential clients than can be given as part of a leaflet or poster. You may need to consider offering workshops or demonstrations in the following situations, each of which will require a slightly different approach:

○ to provide information when the treatment you offer is new or different

○ to attract more clients, if you suspect that they need to see what you are like before choosing to buy a treatment from you.

Specific examples of how they can be used include

○ when you want to introduce your services to doctors, nurses or other practitioners at a local health centre – so that they send you clients

○ when you want to introduce your services to members of staff and clients at a sports or fitness centre – so that staff members will recommend your services and those attending the centre are not only aware of your services, but also know what you can do for them

○ to attract more clients from your target market – for instance you might want to work through local midwives or the National Childbirth Trust contacts if you wish to work with pregnant or post-natal women.

Would-be teachers are advised to consider teacher training courses (run at most adult and further education colleges) and to investigate the rulings of their governing body as to the length of time they should have been practising before beginning to teach. However, those intending to teach on a far less formal basis can make their workshops and demonstrations more successful by following some of the guidelines introduced as part of teacher training. Follow these steps for a successful course:

① Have a plan (sometimes called a lesson plan)

② Make sure you have checked all the resources you need

③ If you are going to use specialist equipment, such as an overhead projector, a flip chart or similar, make sure you have access to it on the day and that you have tested it in advance to see that it works

④ Find out how many participants you are going to have and ensure you have catered for all of them in terms of the number of chairs provided, the number of handouts you supply, any refreshments you are offering, that the size of the room is appropriate and that you have enough equipment if required – things like massage couches for instance

⑤ Ensure that any handouts look professional and are well presented. Check for spelling mistakes and type the handouts where possible. Try to avoid hand-drawn illustrations if you can

⑥ Avoid putting handouts on dark-coloured paper or where it uses small print. This makes them difficult to read and can put off potential clients

⑦ If you can, get someone else to help you with the session by being available to run errands, take a register (if appropriate) or introduce you to the group if they are more familiar with them than you are

⑧ If you use an overhead projector, ensure that you have a screen or large wall to project the image against. Prepare the projector sheets in advance and make sure that you only have a few key phrases on each slide. Don't cram lots of information on one slide, spread it out as this makes things easier to take in

⑨ If you are using a flip chart, you can prepare some of the key things you want to talk about in advance. This will make you look more professional and, if you are new to presenting, will also act as a prompt when you get to this point in the session.

⑩ Run through your session with a friend until you feel confident about what you are saying and how you will say it

⑪ Use prompt cards or notes if you need to. Have them in front of you where you can easily see them if you are worried that you will dry up part

way through. Make sure that these notes or prompt cards are written or typed in large letters so that you can read them easily and the fact that you are using them may not be obvious to the participants.

What does a lesson plan look like?

The lesson plan contains the details of what you are going to do in your class, demonstration or workshop. These are all set out on a step-by-step basis. There are various key elements to the lesson plan, as follows:

○ class details – where it is being held, what time, number of participants

○ lesson aims – these are what you hope to achieve during the session. They might include 'cover benefits of treatment to the participants'. For instance, if you were introducing your treatment to the local health centre, then you might want to ensure that you cover how you can help them to help their patients to better health

○ objectives – these are the things you intend the participants to understand or achieve in the session. Try to make some of them specific to what you want the participants to be able to do at the end of the session. For example, you might want them to be able to explain what the treatment is for or be able to carry out a basic treatment themselves. You might want them to have experienced part of a treatment

○ previous knowledge assumed – what do you believe the participants already know about your services? This should influence how you deliver it. If you think that there will be varying levels of knowledge in the group, you might want to consider starting the session with them telling you what they already know. This can be done very quickly if you ask them to brainstorm the answers

- resources – this is a list of everything you need to make the session work. Include all equipment, references to handouts you will need to provide, and so on

- action – this is the longest section of the lesson plan and gives details of the time allocated to each activity taking place, what the tutor (you) is doing at any time and what the participants are doing. The action section might look something like this:

Time	Content	Tutor activity	Participant activity
10.00–10.10	Introduction and welcome	Tutor presentation	Listening
10.10–10.20	What would we like to achieve by trying complementary therapies/recommending them to our clients?	Writing participants' responses on flip chart, encouraging additional responses	Brainstorming, offering suggestions

DEFINITION

Brainstorming – means that you ask a question where there are several possible answers and participants will offer suggestions. Write down everything they say, so that they see that any response is acceptable, this encourages all participants to join in. You can then sum up the key points you want to concentrate on at the end of the session.

How do you make a workshop effective and exciting?

FOR DISCUSSION

Think back to your own training in your chosen disciplines as well as to any other learning experiences you have had. What classes do you particularly remember? What was it about them that worked?

Teacher training emphasises the need for teachers to adopt a variety of different activities in the classroom so that you can change the pace of the presentation and provide different ways of learning things. Complementary therapies are at an advantage when it comes to presentations as most people attending a workshop will be interested in the practical side of the work and trying it out themselves. If you have got them to the workshop, you need to sustain their interest. Here are some techniques that you might want to consider as part of any workshop you do. Don't feel obliged to use all of them – some won't work with different kinds of groups!

Method	Advantages	Disadvantages
Lecture or tutor presentation	Can get a large amount of material across in a short space of time. Easy to prepare for. Best if you have a charismatic delivery style and support it with visual material such as overheads, frequent breaks, lots of examples and introduce other techniques as well.	Can't always tell if the participants are listening to you.
Brainstorming	Less formal, builds rapport and participation quickly. Good at the start of a session or as a summary exercise.	Depends on participation, if students don't join in, this won't work. Can look unprepared. Tutor needs to be quick with the pen and taking notes on the flip chart.
Question/answer – asking questions of the participants and waiting for an answer from them. Also can offer a chance for participants to ask the tutor	Useful at checking whether they understand what you have been talking about. Can indicate where interest lies for student. Can change pace of session. Encourages everyone to concentrate on the question and on what they know in case they are asked something.	Be careful not to ask these too quickly or give the answer before participants have had a chance to think about it.
Demonstration	Necessary to introduce practical skills. Visually more interesting to the participants. Participants can go over key aspects they aren't sure of. Must be supported with step-by-step handouts to act as reminders to the students.	All participants need a clear view of the demonstration. One demonstration may not be enough, follow up with other demonstrations if you need to develop the skills of the participants.
Guided practicals	Once you have demonstrated a skill, you could use these to make sure that each student is going through the practical element at the same pace and that each one is working correctly before moving on.	Only necessary if you are teaching a short course.
Pair work	Participants get to work closely with one other delegate before feeding back to the larger group, this is less threatening for self-conscious individuals.	Can take a lot of time to get feedback from each pair in a large group. Works best with small- to medium-sized groups.

Method	Advantages	Disadvantages
Small group work (threes or fours)	Can extend the pair work, allowing more discussion. Still not too threatening. Easy to use. Allows participants to look at a particular area of interest in more depth. Tutor can provide specialised support. Changes pace of the class.	
Worksheets	Allow participants to go at their own pace. You can provide extra information above and beyond what you actually talk about. Can provide step-by-step instruction, so participants keep going even if they don't have your full attention at the time.	Be careful that you don't produce too many handouts! Keep them relevant to what you intend to cover.
Snowballing – starting an exercise with small groups or pairs then bringing two or more groups together as a next step prior to whole class work	Exercise is not threatening to begin with and gradually gets participants used to joining in the group.	Can take a lot of time, more useful when you are running a short course than if it is a one-day workshop or shorter.
Discovery – involves participants learning through the use of more than one sense – such as touch, sight, taste, smell or hearing	Very useful if you are introducing products or equipment to participants (for instance essential oils). Could follow demonstrations or take their place.	Can be time consuming May not relate in an obvious way to the point of the workshop.
Group discussion	Introduces the participants' own experience. Can be very interesting to all concerned. Will link into question/answer sessions. Encourages networking and builds rapport between participants.	Difficult to control the length and direction that the discussion takes. Need to ensure that you remind participants of the key issues covered by the discussion. Can lead into hot topics (where emotions could run high) if you aren't careful.
Debate	Works best with very able participants who know their subject matter. Can be very lively and interactive. When handled well will be amusing.	Requires participants to be thoroughly prepared beforehand, be able or willing to talk in an informed manner and be able or willing to present the views of one argument (even if they don't necessarily hold those views).

Method	Advantages	Disadvantages
Role play	Highly interactive, very lively (as long as the participants are willing to engage with the material). Needs time for preparation and for participants to ask questions and receive guidance about how this would work.	Requires imagination, willingness to participate, needs some preparation to make it work well, work best when the participants have some knowledge about the materials or ideas covered by the role play or if they are already familiar with the group and willing to engage in this kind of activity.
Games	Useful revision tools, can be amusing, could include word searches or crosswords or similar. Best supported by clear instructions.	Not the easiest, or most time-effective, method to use as part of the workshop. May need some explanations as to the rules of the game. Participants who prefer a formal education experience won't enjoy these.
Presentation/feedback	Useful if you have carried out small group work – getting the participants to feed back what they have discovered to the other members of the group.	Time consuming. Ensure you provide clear guidance about how long the participant needs to speak for and to what level. No guarantees about outcome.

The following are some of the things you might want to use to support any workshops you do, with reasons for and against using them

Teaching Aid	Advantages	Disadvantages
Whiteboard/markers	Focus students' attention on key issues. Can be used to scribe or during brainstorming exercises effectively. Can illustrate topics under current discussion. Can be used to provide a visual format for the content of the lesson – helping students to make connections.	Can't keep what is written for future reference or to revisit a topic at a later date. Can't refer back during the same lesson if the material has already been removed from the board. If not properly cleaned, markers can have difficulty working effectively.

Teaching Aid	Advantages	Disadvantages
OHTs	Very useful if you have a large class and a lot of information to cover. Handouts can be exact replicas of the OHTs, making it easier for the students to follow the lesson and add notes to the relevant sheets. Full colour available. Tidier – if teacher has messy handwriting.	Need to be carefully organised. You can't diverge easily from the planned presentation. Will need other media as back up if students ask complicated questions that require illustration and you haven't prepared enough to answer them.
Flip charts	Information covered is easy to keep so that you can refer back to what has been previously covered.	Messy. Difficult to store. Can't be used with a large class (difficult to see at the back of the room).
Powerpoint/computer presentations	Full colour available. Can include complex diagrams if needed. Handouts can incorporate all slides produced and/or space for additional notes. Looks professional.	Power failures or problems with the computer can make this difficult to use. You can't diverge easily from the planned presentation (answering student's queries unless planned). Requires adequate computer support and facilities to display the projection.
Slides	Flexible format – you can rearrange the order if you need to change your presentation. Focusses student's attention. Visually stimulating. Works best alongside other resources, to enhance visual aspects.	Equipment must be regularly serviced and in good working order. Often regarded as outdated – expensive to maintain. Darkened room can encourage the students to fall asleep if they aren't fully motivated.
Handouts/worksheets	Personalised service and information for the students, taking into consideration the needs of the course and their particular learning styles. Can include background reading. Helps students review key issues from the lesson.	Large photocopying bill. Relies on student to read and absorb the material.
Realia	Visually stimulating. Makes the subject matter come to life. Can generate fascinating tasks and lively discussion.	Can be difficult or expensive to source. Can be difficult to store.
Models	Must be simple to use and operate. Must be applicable to the subject matter – and able to simplify a complex topic. Must be properly planned and introduced, so students see the relevance of the model to the work at hand.	Can be expensive or time-consuming if not handled properly.

Teaching Aid	Advantages	Disadvantages
Tape recorders	Useful for students who have difficulty following the lesson – for instance when English is their second language or when they are visually impaired.	Sound can be disturbed, tapes wasted if there is irrelevant material or discussion taking place. Need regular monitoring.
Videos/movies/film	Useful if the material covered is immediately relevant and useful to the students and to the topic being covered. Require introduction by the tutor so that the students are aware of the reasons for viewing. Visually stimulating. Tutor needs to monitor the video and stop it at intervals for discussion to take place and to emphasise the key learning points. Better for a longer course, not a short workshop.	Special equipment required. Enough time to watch the material is required. Equipment that both works and is ready prior to the class is required. Tutor familiarity with the equipment (and preparation beforehand, so that they know the video will start at the right place on time) all required. If equipment fails, back-up plans must be in place.

TASK

Prepare all aspects of a presentation that you would make to either your local health centre (doctors, nurses, midwives and physiotherapists) or your local sports centre (members of staff and members of the public). Your presentation pack should include:

○ *details of who you expect the participants to be, what you think their key concerns are and what you think they will want to hear about your services*

○ *a lesson plan, complete with the resources you would need to run it*

○ *all handouts that you feel these groups would want to see*

○ *a leaflet or poster promoting the presentation (if going to the sports centre)*

○ *an outline of other workshops, talks or presentations that you could carry out to follow on from your initial presentation (for instance, you might want to offer additional sessions to the health practice on how your treatment is of particular use in aiding certain conditions).*

Expert Witness: Introducing a New Product into a New and Existing Market

Astrid Kauffmann practises Aromatherapy, Reiki, and Spiritual Healing as well as working with the Bach flower remedy system. For the past five years she has also been practising Jin Shin Jyutsu and is one of only 40–50 practitioners in the UK who work with this art. Astrid describes Jin Shin Jyutsu as the art of harmonising the life energy of the body. Deceptively simple in the way it can be applied, she has found the effects of the treatment and the benefits to her clients to be quite profound. Because it is so different from any other treatment process currently available, explaining it to potential clients has been 'interesting'! Astrid says that her past experiences working in advertising and doing desk top design work for investment banking organisations has helped her immensely as she promotes her work.

" Having transferable skills has been really important in introducing Jin Shin Jyutsu to people as I needed the confidence and experience of doing presentations in order to know how to be clear when communicating and to be able to stand up in front of an audience. The desk top publishing has also been a real asset, as being able to produce all my own advertising and marketing materials at home means that I have been able to cut down on the amount of time involved in producing a flier, that I don't have to depend on anyone else to get the flier out and that I am able to respond to suggestions from clients or colleagues and adapt my leaflets easily. When you are introducing a new product to people, you really do need to be flexible and be prepared to try all different ideas. Being able to produce my leaflets and posters on demand – as opportunities arise – has been a real bonus.

continued...

Expert Witness: Introducing a New Product into a New and Existing Market

continued...

In general, Jin Shin Jyutsu is at an interesting stage as it doesn't yet mean much to most clients. Although it is a form of energetic treatment that specialises in self-help techniques, that is just the tip of the iceberg in explaining how it works. I've had to introduce it through my Aromatherapy so that it is linked to something people already know and, in effect, it has become part of what makes my treatment unique. I use Jin Shin Jyutsu as part of the consultation process and as home care and after care so that I can tailor the treatment to focus on the client's needs more precisely.

What this means is that I am continually promoting Jin Shin Jyutsu in new ways and I can't rely on any of the traditional methods of promotion – like advertising or even leaflets as they don't always get across the information needed to help people decide if this is the right thing for them. Advertising might work in the future, but at the moment there is so little awareness of what Jin Shin Jyutsu does that it would be a total waste of time. I prefer word of mouth and am always carrying leaflets with me and talking about what I do every chance I get. People need to see how excited you are by the techniques in order to be willing to try it out themselves.

continued...

Workshops and demonstrations are far more effective, and I believe what makes these work is my enthusiasm for what I am talking about. Those who are attending are usually people who have either experienced Jin Shin Jyutsu directly themselves and want to know more or who have got excited from hearing someone talk about it who has experienced it already. Not everyone who comes to a workshop will become a client, however. People seem to arrive at a workshop for one of two reasons – either they are at a crossroads in their lives (or dealing with some trauma, which could include physical or emotional stress) or they are there out of general interest. Usually it is the former group who are more likely to become clients. The latter group is often more interested in picking up the very powerful self-help tips Jin Shin Jyutsu offers.

I am not particularly worried about whether people convert from the workshops to becoming clients as at this stage I have my other therapies to help bring in the money. It is more important with the Jin Shin Jyutsu that I remain flexible and go where there is a demand for treatments or workshops. What this does mean is that I am now working in Greater London, Wiltshire and Somerset – all areas where there are a lot of therapists practising more mainstream complementary treatments, where clients are aware and interested in work related to the meridians and where complementary health centres are now looking for something new and specialised to offer as part of their services. Finding interested, aware clients seems to be a real key to the success of the business.

continued...

I really feel that Jin Shin Jyutsu will become the bulk of my work in the future, although there is still a great deal of promotion and work that I need to carry out to make this happen. I think my next step must be to work at getting some articles about it published, so that people start to become more aware of this discipline. Whilst I have the passion and willingness to persevere to make this work, sometimes it can be disheartening to see how slowly things and people move, even those who are aware of the effects of energetic treatments and are committed to working with them. Don't expect immediate results if you are introducing a existing product into a new market let alone a new one into a new market!

What I have found useful, which I didn't to start off with when I first qualified as a therapist, is to have a vision of what I want to achieve within five years. Putting that into place meant that I could now see where I was going, even if I am being flexible about how I am going to get there. That's why I am introducing the Jin Shin Jyutsu as part of a special kind of Aromatherapy treatment for the moment, adding a new product to an existing market, even though my intention is introduce Jin Shin Jyutsu on its own later. **"**

Checking your understanding

Refer to the Expert Witness Case Study for the first four questions

1. What stage of the product life cycle is Jin Shin Jyutsu in?

2. Think about the Boston Matrix. What category does Jin Shin Jyutsu fall into? Where do you think Astrid would place her aromatherapy treatments?

3. Astrid describes the people who are most likely to try her treatments as being aware of energetic work, possibly at a crossroads in their lives or dealing with some form of physical or emotional trauma. What clients would you suggest she targets? How would she find them?

4. If Astrid were attempting to promote her services, and Jin Shin Jyutsu in general, through media in your area (either magazines, newspapers, radio, or television), which particular magazines, newspaper?

5. What is meant by the product life cycle?

6. What signs would you look for that might indicate it is time for you to alter the way you promote your business or to seek new clients (consider in relation to the product life cycle)

7. What is meant by a cash cow? Give an example from your own experiences.

8. Explain the advantages and disadvantages of having two services – one of which is a problem child and one of which is a star as part of your business. What can you do to change this?

9. You have been asked to develop a three-hour workshop for stressed business executives based around your treatment services. Design the workshop, including a lesson plan, any equipment requirements, a promotional poster and any handouts you would require.

10. Produce a list of interview questions that you expect you would be asked if you were applying for a job on a cruise ship.

UK Government support agencies

Enterprise Advisory Service (for government grants and assistance for business)
www.govgrants.com

Local government information services
www.info4local.gov.uk

About taxes
www.inlandrevenue.gov.uk

Business Link (England)
Tel. 0845 756 7765

Business Connect (Wales)
Tel. 0845 796 9798

Scottish Small Business Gateway
Tel. 0141 221 5513

LEDU (Northern Ireland)
Tel. 028 9049 1031

Uniforms, Towels, etc

DK Profashion
Tel. 01732 359789

Buttercups Career Wear
Lonsdale House
Avoca Ave
Blackrock
Co. Dublin
Ireland
buttercupsuniforms@iolfree.ie

MontaguDesign Work Wear
151 Northfield Avenue
London
W13 9QT
Tel. 020 8567 1368
www.montagugroup.co.uk

Duncan Stewart Textiles
Aztex House
Ivy Arch Rd
Worthing
West Sussex
BN14 8BX
Tel. 01903 201 251

Majestic Towels Ltd
Majestic House
72 Alfred Street
Sparkbrook
Birmingham
B12 8JP
www.majestictowels.co.uk

Ellisons Beauty Suppliers
43 Bayton Road
Exhall
Coventry
CV7 9EF
Tel. 01203 761619

Treatment equipment/couches

New Concept
www.new-concept.co.uk
Tel. 01473 721559

Beautelle
www.beautelle.co.uk
Tel. 01384 76665

Marshcouch
www.marshcouch.com
Tel. 01442 263199

Bellissima
www.beautyequipment.co.uk
Tel. 0161 976 4614

About health issues and products

Miscellaneous websites

www.thinknatural.com

www.naturesbestonline.com

www.healthreaction.com

www.baldwins.co.uk

www.positivehealthshop.co.uk

www.vitaminsandhealth.co.uk

www.herbalnetco.uk

www.boots-plc.com

www.essentiallyoils.com

www.quinessence.com

www.nutrient.co.uk

www.ukhealthguide.co.uk

Ainsworths (homeopathic products and advice)

Tel. 0207 935 5330

Insurance information

www.bupa.co.uk

HSBC Gibbs Insurance brokers

Tel. 01444 313244

Complementary therapies support agencies

Miscellaneous websites

www.massagetherapy.co.uk

www.yogatherapy.org

www.acupuncture.org.uk

www.therapyindex.com

International Federation of Professional Aromatherapists

www.ifpaaroma.org

www.itecworld.co.uk

National Institute of Medical Herbalists

www.nimh.org.uk

Complementary Medical Association

www.the-cma.org.uk

Association of Reflexologists

www.aor.org.uk